The Bitter Bitch Chronicles

Life with Difficult Coworkers

Ms. Sinn D. Rella

Early Praise for *the Bitter Bitch Chronicles*

Sinn D. Rella has truly captured the core of the bad civil-service worker. Her experience illustrates how one bad employee can make coming to work so much worse for everyone else. Her tips for preventing catching the BB virus are keys to promoting healthy, happy work spaces. She does all of this with a lightheartedness and sense of humor lacking from other books in this genre. I wish The BB Chronicles *had been out when I was running an agency!*

~Rebecca E. Blanton, Former Executive Director,
California Commission on the Status of Women and Girls

As a debut novel, the Bitter Bitches Chronicles is hilarious and a compulsively relatable read and Sinn D. Rella is spot on in her assessment of that little bit of bitter in us all. Her years of performing comedy are evident in this laugh of loud-trip-back to the why of it.

~Kat Bowers, Comedian, Writer

The Bitter Bitch Chronicles: Life with Difficult Coworkers

Sinn D. Rella and Liquid Courage

© 2017

Cover Illustration and page illustrations by: Kul Black

Photos reproduced with permissions by:

"Jungle Cube" Photo by Sinn D. Rella

"Bitches in the Mist" Photo by Sinn D. Rella

"Ain't got time for that" Photo by Sinn D, Rella

"Disability" Photo by Sinn D. Rella

"Let it go" Photo by Sinn D. Rella

"It's Lonely Up There" Photo by Rebecca E. Blanton

"Poisoned tea" Photo by Rebecca E. Blanton

Author photo by: Kul Black

ISBN: 978-0-692922460

         0692922466

Printed By: CreateSpace

Contact Sinn D. Rella at: MsRella@me.com

To All You Bitter Bitches Out There,

If I hadn't met you, if you hadn't decorated your cubicles
with troll dolls, cat photos, desk toys, and more crap than
any office has ever needed, I wouldn't have my career in
comedy—or this book.

I hope you all find happiness somewhere and don't get
eaten by your cats when you die.

~ Sinn

Preface

I loved writing this book, even though it took me

years to put it together. I always had the thoughts

in my head, but putting them on paper was a task

that was unbearable, like trying to spread peanut butter on soft bread; it tears a lot, but eventually you might end up with a sandwich.

I have spent decades dealing with people I call Bitter Bitches. These are people who are miserable and work to bring their misery into your life. I wish I had some magical solution for the Bitter Bitch syndrome, but I don't. What I can say is that we need to try to get along and sometimes agree to disagree. There are times in life when we need to realize that growing up means learning when to shut up. We need to take a step back sometimes and just look over the situation at hand before stepping in with high emotions.

I know for certain that the tongue is a very dangerous tool. It can cut down the high and mighty and lift up the weak. One thing for sure:

once the words are out, there are no take-backs. You can apologize, but it will always be on the person's mind—because at one time it was on yours. I have this fifteen-second rule; sometimes it works, and sometimes it doesn't. I try not to say the negative thing that's on my mind right away. I try to hold it in for fifteen seconds. If in fifteen seconds I feel the same way, I will say it.

I have only recently adopted this rule, later in my life. Maybe if I had applied this rule in my twenties, thirties, and some of my forties, I would have a few more friends. Maybe, maybe not. I'm really not trying to make too many more friends. I have learned the title "friend" is a special word reserved for people I really like. Now the other people I meet are in a group entitled "acquaintances?" I will call you and talk and share a few things, but you are not the person I would call if I need bail money or if I need your help *before* I need the bail money. The people I'd call at such times are the ones I call friends.

Throughout life you meet people who fall into different categories. *Friend* is the highest category you can have. You share things: the good, bad, and ugly. Friends are there when you need them, regardless of the reason. You are not scared to call them when you're in need. The need can be emotional, and they are there not to judge but to help.

Work can be a place to meet true friends, but it is also a place to be wary of people who call themselves true friends. I have met a few people at work who became true friends, but I knew almost instantly that they were true people. The ones who are phony showed their colors within a few weeks.

I knew I wanted no part of them, and I did not want them in my life. They were bitter: bitter about things that were totally uncontrollable and out of step with their concept of life.

Everybody is not happy to see you happy. You may have so-called friends you want to share your joy with, but you know they are not actually happy to see you happy. They'd rather see you bitter and unhappy, as they are. They do not want to see you in a happy place, mainly because they are not happy. After all, misery loves company. "Just as people love to share their joy, others are Bitter Bitches, lurking around the corner, waiting to suck the joy out of everyone else." Just when you're ready to share your joy, some Bitter Bitch is lurking around the corner, waiting to suck the joy right out of you. Talk about the new-car experience!

Everybody has struggles. "My struggles are no easier or more difficult than yours, no more or less important than yours." It always depends on how we handle the struggle—or how the struggle handles us.

Sinn D. Rella
Sacramento, California
November 2016

TABLE OF CONTENTS

Introduction

*M*any of us are deeply unhappy with our job. Our

dissatisfaction may stem from unpleasant interactions with

our boss, coworkers, or customers. While many of us have

the ability to compartmentalize our dissatisfaction and not

spread it around the office, the Bitter Bitch (BB) fails to do

this. Rather, BBs excel at making their personal

dissatisfaction an issue for as many people as possible in

the office. Our interactions with BBs at work lead to our

own unhappiness in the workplace.

BBs excel at spreading their bad attitude around to

coworkers, and it spreads throughout the office faster than

word of hot Krispy Kreme donuts in the break room. The

BB's poor attitude infects the office like a virus. The BB

manifests a bad attitude, poor customer service, passive-

aggressive behavior with coworkers and staff, and

performance that is just enough to keep a job but still results in coworkers picking up her slack.

The BB takes her bad attitude out of the office and into the larger world. We see this manifest as road rage, violence, and rudeness. For example, when the Bitter Bitch goes to the grocery story, she will huff and puff while standing in line for the cashier like the rest of the customers. The BB takes the necessity of waiting for service as a personal affront.

I meet Bitter Bitches everywhere. BB native habitats include the grocery store, carwash, theaters, schools, hospitals, airports, banks, and even churches. Yes, advanced cases of BB virus lead BBs to even take that attitude into houses of worship, where they are supposed to be grateful as they celebrate the Lord. Instead, BBs are super annoyed at the second passing of the collection plate for the food-pantry fund. They are everywhere. Everywhere! Seriously, I mean *everywhere.*

Bitter Bitches contaminate the entire office with the BB virus. The BB virus is actually more virulent than the common cold, but unlike the cold, contracting the BB virus leads to increased time at work and an increased need to infect all coworkers. Like a succubus, the BB sucks all the joy out of you in the first ten minutes of your work shift. The BB's sole source of joy comes from schadenfreude—delighting in the misery of others. The goal of every BB is to make as many fellow coworkers as deeply dissatisfied with the office as she is.

I've had over twenty jobs in the past thirty-five years of my career, and I can remember only *one* I was happy to go to each day. I have long been aware of the problems of the BB, and I've always tried my hardest not to be bitter as I go into work. In my mind—and possibly actually at work—I kept a good attitude, but I'm sure there were days when I was a BB in action.

If you have never met a BB, I have sad news for you: you actually do know a BB—and it's *you.*

We all encounter Bitter Bitches in our work. While we easily can recognize this person these people, male or female, dealing with them and limiting the impact of their negativity is much more difficult. My lifelong experience with BBs puts me in a supremely strong position to offer suggestions for dealing with the BB's in your life. I draw on my experience working in the private industry and, government work, navigating the disability system, and working as a comic to provide illustrations of BB's, describe their impact on the world, and offer practical suggestions for dealing with BB's.

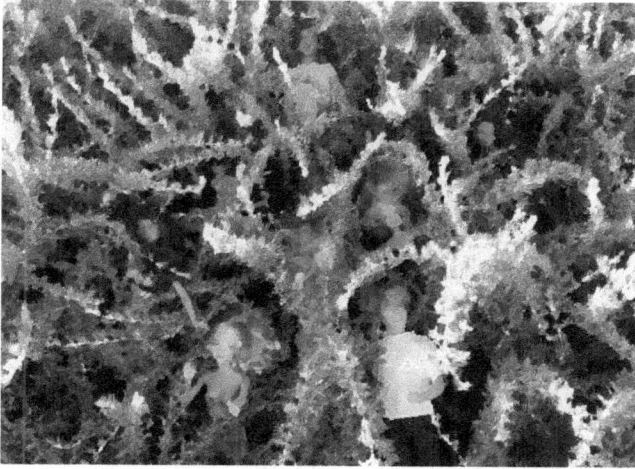

Chapter 1: Bitches in the Mist

*T*he Bitter Bitch is one who possesses a bad attitude for no

particular reason. A BB exudes so much negativity a blind

person can see it.

Bitter Bitches are not just women. I have encountered a

number of men who qualify as BBs (also called BBPs—BBs

with a Penis). Bitter Bitches are disgruntled all the time and

bring that attitude to work. Their attitude is so bad you can

see their unhappiness as soon as they get out of their car.

You watch them pull into the parking lot. They sit in their car longer than can possibly be necessary, packing up their bags with personal effects to decorate their cube, plant food for the green monstrosity they have grown, and condiments to stock their personal mini-fridge they fought management for the right to put under their desk, and they douse themselves with some scent that only BBs seem to be able to find at Ross. The walk from the lot to the office resembles something from *The Walking Dead.* You see the horror coming but cannot escape the inevitable interaction.

> *Patience is one form of inoculation against the Bitter Bitch virus.*

BBs find small, passive-aggressive ways to spread their bad attitude. You greet them with "Good morning," and they reply, "Is it really?" I try to inoculate myself from the BB virus. I practice starting my day with a good attitude. If I don't start the day with a good attitude, the rest of the day will be bad. BBs, on the other hand, pride themselves in elevating the negative. I am willing to bet that even during yoga, the BB's mantra is "Ommhh...fuck this."

I learned early in life that I need a lot of patience and prayer to deal with coworkers and clients with bad attitudes. Patience is one form of inoculation against the BB virus. The capacity and skill to cope with difficult people came to me with time, age, and experience.

Inexperienced and younger coworkers tend to express themselves quickly and graphically. What they fail to see is: 1) doing so will not change the BB, and 2) having a hair trigger will get them fired. I'm not saying you must always hold your tongue, but there is a time and place to express yourself. As a general rule, the workplace is not the appropriate place for a tongue-lashing.

When Your Coworker Is a Bitter Bitch

At most jobs there is that one employee who has been in the same position, the same department, the same unit, and the same cubicle forever. Forever! I mean for-ev-er. His or her cubicle has taken on the unique and unfortunate personality of the bitter person.

I encountered employees like this while working for the State of California and the City of San Francisco. These employees had been there so long they can could tell you about the days when you were allowed to actually smoke at your desk. Wow! You know that was a long time ago. I am not exaggerating here. I worked with a woman who still kept an ashtray on her desk like, as if waiting for the second coming of Philip Morris.

Some of these employees are valuable because of their wealth of knowledge. It is not that BBs have no value. They may have knowledge, but the BB virus has made it nearly impossible for them to use this knowledge constructively. The amazing thing to me is that many BBs I have encountered had the option of retiring or changing jobs, yet they stayed planted in their current job. I often wondered why, because I'm sure there were many opportunities for promotions to move on, yet they remained in that same cubicle. The refusal to move on made me wonder what their home life must have been like. I think many times employees like them opt for the misery they know rather than risk the unknown of happiness and fulfillment. Change is scary and difficult to deal with. Change can mean dealing with new people, new things, and a new job.

They stay either because of the fear of change or the fact that packing up their cubicle would require a professional moving staff. Many times these employees have cubicles that are filled to the brim with junk. They are hoarders. Their space is filled with pictures of kids from birth to marriage. They have pictures of three generations of their cats. They have enough condiments to stock the average hotdog cart. And there is so much junk in their computer hard drive that excavating it would reveal dead LOLcats.

The only positive thing about this hoarding is that they always have Tylenol, Excedrin, Midol, Nyquil, Band-Aid, nail clippers, clear nail polish, a miniature sewing kit, extra buttons, a set of extra bathroom keys, and trinkets to give your kids on random holidays you forgot to buy gifts for. They are the Walgreens Pharmacy of the office. They have made that cubicle their home.

BBs are people who seem to choose to stay in a miserable position because the knowledge of the daily drudgery is almost comforting. What bothers me is that BBs become annoyed, angry, or vindictive when other people exercise an option to move forward with their life.

When Your Supervisor Is Bitter

Some supervisors are supervisors because they were presented with the opportunity, failed at it, and nobody wanted to admit the promotion was a mistake, so the supervisors retained their position. Many of the supervisors I worked for while I was employed with the State of California were appallingly bad at the job. They held the position only because they were next available on the state-certified list. The State offered supervisory training courses, but these employees clearly had not exercised the option of taking the classes.

Most of the supervisors I worked with were BBs. I found out that these people were bitter either because they had no life or they were not in control of the life they had. They had a need to come into the workplace and order people around to be in control of something. They used their position as a way of bullying employees into doing things.

Bitter supervisors arrive early and leave late. It is not that they are dedicated to their work. More often, it is because their home life is a disaster. Many times these are the people who never take a vacation and never call in sick. They think the workplace cannot function without them.

These are the supervisors who will come into the job on Saturday because they were driving by the building. They consider it a virtue to never leave the office. Sick? Going to infect the whole office? They think I will come in anyway, because it shows dedication! They can develop ulcers and hair loss and anger issues, but damned if they will take a vacation day! Little do they know we are all cheering for their retirement. Yes! Retire! Please go—and do you need me to hire a U-Haul to get your cube home to your overstuffed garage?

BB supervisors have some telltale behaviors. I had a supervisor who would single out an employee and ride that employee until she would quit or leave the unit because of stress-related problems. The supervisor would nitpick everything the employee did. The supervisor would watch the clock and mark the employee late if she was not at her desk within three minutes of the designated start time. Typos in the employee's work were treated like an assault on the supervisor. Asking for time off to go to the doctor was an unforgivable sin that HR forced the supervisor to live with.

This type of supervisory skillset does not benefit anyone. Riding an employee for being one or two minutes late has a trickle-down effect of ensuring a bad attitude among other employees. I'm not saying excessive tardiness is acceptable. However, being petty about a few minutes increases stress and leads employees to start the day with a bad attitude. If you are in a foul mood by 8:02 a.m., it leads to bad behavior and negativity in the office. Other employees pick up on this negativity, and it ultimately causes the entire office to be affected by the Bitter Bitch virus.

I recognize this bitter-supervisor behavior because I had a bosshole who would come in early and leave late. She never took a vacation and rarely called in sick. I don't know if she was going for employee of the year or just liked being a nuisance. I do know most of the staff despised her.

She had a reputation for being very sneaky. Her version of supervision was to treat all employees as if they were prisoners. This would be appropriate if we were in prison— but we were not. We were just doing hard time under her command. She would come in early to harass the employees who were late.

Never mind that we didn't have to punch a time clock. She would stay late to make sure the employees who came in late did not leave early. Under her rule, putting in a seven-hour-and-fifty-two-minute day was considered sloth and theft from the company. I gave her the nickname Secret Squirrel. She would go through my desk when I was not there. I would leave her notes in my desk like, "What are you looking for in here? It's not here. Check the desk in the corner." I loved leaving notes because I knew she could not say anything; really, she had no business in my desk. This supervisor created an environment that made all the employees bitter about their jobs because of the unnecessary pressures she put on the workers.

Self-Care When You Work with Bitter Bitches

Maintaining your sanity while working with Bitter Bitches is an important skill to surviving any workplace. BBs will draw you into their world, and you will manifest bad behaviors and attitudes. You can find yourself doing stupid things in response to their petty behaviors: things like playing chicken with answering the phone. The person to break first and pick up the receiver is the loser. Petty people have a way of drawing you into acting out stupid behaviors. Most of the petty stuff we do at the office comes from dealing with Bitter Bitches.

We tend to lose our manners when we deal with BBs. Employees working with BBs will try to maintain office etiquette and not fall into their world of bitterness. The longer this continues, the more difficult it becomes. Manners and etiquette take muscle and discipline. And like all muscles, the "polite" muscle can grow fatigued—and when it does, you collapse into bitterness.

As much as I have fought the BB virus, I have caught myself not talking to a coworker because another coworker was angry with her. Then I realized this was a place of business and I was at work. I knew we were not in high school and should be adults. Why add more tension to a situation that was already filled with tension? Ultimately, I recognized my bad behavior and said "Hello" to this ostracized coworker. A simple hello can go a long way to fighting the BB virus.

18: J.O.B.S.

Employment Application

Programs, services and employment are equally available to everyone. Please inform the Human Resources Department if you require reasonable accommodation for the application or interview.

Date of Interview (Month/Day/Year): / /

Applicant Data

Position Applied for:

How were you referred to us: My COUSIN BubA

Full Name: Betty Bitter

Address: 18 Resentful Road City: Crabbyville State: Zip:

Phone: NO   Mobile/Pager/Other: After my 1st check E-mail: refer to previous answer

Date Available to Start: Tomorrow   Social Security Number: Yes.   Salary Requirements: Yes

If you are under 18 years of age, can you provide a work permit? ☐ Yes ☐ No   If no, please explain:

Have you ever worked for this company? ☑ Yes ☐ No   If yes, when? When I show up

Are you legally allowed to work in the United States? ☑ Yes ☐ No   Today I can

Type of employment desired: ☐ Full-Time ☑ Part-Time ☑ Temporary ☑ Seasonal

Have you ever pleaded guilty, no contest or been convicted of a crime? ☐ Yes ☐ No   If yes, give dates and details:

Answering yes to these questions does not constitute an automatic rejection for employment. Date of the offense, seriousness and nature of the violation, rehabilitation and position applied for will be considered.

Driver's license number (if applicable to position):   State:

Education History

Name & Location of High School: High high school HighLAND   Did you graduate? UNsure

Name & Location of College: Yale University New Haven, CT   Years attended: Yes

Degrees completed: Yes   Other Subjects Studied:

Trade, Business or Correspondence School: Office Personality School   Years attended:

Subjects Studied: Bitteology 101, I hate work 204   Did you graduate: Yes

Summarize Your Special Skills or Qualifications

Dodge ball champ of Mrs. Walkers 3rd grade class. Kickball champs of Mr. Adams 4th grade class. Most likely to improve of the 7th grade. I do not work well with others and I hate working on the phones

Chapter 2: J.O.B.S.—

Working for a Living

I have never been a morning person. The work world,

unfortunately, does not cater to me. I learned early that six

a.m. was the start of a workday. OMG! I would have loved to

sleep in so many mornings; my warm bed was so seductive.

Many of my positions required me to drag myself from a

blanket's warm embrace and go adult.

Fortunately, not every position requires an early call time,

and being early is not the only way to succeed in the

business world. I realized early in my career that the early

bird gets the worm and the second mouse gets the cheese.

It is important to be smart about your career decisions.

Sometimes this means setting a second alarm to assure you

are up and awake. Sometimes it means figuring out

creative ways to deal with work-world realities. Much of this insight did not come to me until after a few years on the job.

My Fairytale First Job

I had no expectations about work at age fifteen. I could barely define the word expectations. All I knew was work was something my dad and mom did, and it paid cash every other week. I had no idea you had to deal with people and the real world! My world up to that point was pretty small. I was a happy kid, and when I dreamed of a job, I thought that work would also lead to happiness.

It was the '70s, and most kids attended summer school or worked. I never thought I could coast through summers without working. I actually looked forward to getting my first job.

What I did not realize was that work is a life sentence of hard labor. I did not think about a job (or jobs) lasting a lifetime. I found out that I would always have to work. All my adult life. With the realization that I would be lucky to get two weeks off a year for the next forty years of dragging myself into the office, the idea of work became daunting. If I was lucky, I would work for decades, then get old and tired and die. Yay?

I got my first job at age fifteen at the Children's Fairyland in Oakland, California. Fairyland has been a staple theme park in the area for more than fifty years now. When I started working there, the place was over twenty years old and really look liked it.

Most people who grew up in the Bay Area know Fairyland well. Fairyland is a theme park based on classic fairytales and is broken up into areas for Humpty Dumpty, the Old Lady in the Shoe, the Old Maid, etc. Each of these areas has a key box. You insert a purchased plastic key into the box, and a recorded story plays. Keys are good forever. Really. Forever—or as long as Fairyland is in existence.

My first job! What an adventure! I was happy to land this job. It was the summer of 1975 in Oakland. Summer brought warm days, cool nights, and promises of a lot of fun. The thought of having my own money really excited me. I dreamed of cars, shoes, and saying, "I can buy that!"

I was happy. The job was slated to last six weeks, which seemed like a good introduction to the working world. Every day I woke up early, excited to start my work at Fairyland. I worked from eight a.m. to noon five days a week. That was a schedule I could live with—and fantasized about after I got more permanent positions.

My mom would drop me off in the morning, and I would head in to Fairyland to get my assignment for the day. My primary duty was stocking food for the animals that lived at Fairyland. I used to count out sardines, place them in waxed paper bags, and insert the bags into a machine for the public to purchase. I did this for two hours, and then I stocked the birdseed. This kept me busy, and I enjoyed the job because I knew I was getting paid for my services.

There were no hand sanitizers and no OSHA rules other than wash your hands when you finished work. Even without the "wash your hands" rule, I would have done so. I smelled like sardines by noon every day. When work was over, I would wash my hands, walk to the corner of Lakeshore Boulevard, and catch the bus home and think about my day. All the way home, the smell of anchovies wafted from my hands and filled my thoughts. I am sure that is why the seat next to me was always empty. The fishy smell still curls through my nostrils and drips down my throat when I think about it today.

Who would suspect a job that left me smelling of anchovies would be one of my favorite work memories?

This job had key elements that made it a great job. There was no pressure. My duties were clearly defined: stock the fish and birdseed machines, take a break, work within a delineated timeframe. This job did not require me to stay eight hours. This job did not require me to get along with people. This job required no real skills. The duration of the job was limited. There was no pressure. I liked this job a lot.

The first surprise I encountered in the work world involved the necessity of delayed gratification. Payday was every two weeks, and it seemed like forever between checks. When I started my job, no one told me that I needed to work two weeks before a check would be issued and that it would take *another* two weeks to get my check!

When my first payday arrived, I remember waiting anxiously for my check. I was informed that I had to wait two weeks for processing before I would receive any money. WHAT?! I didn't get a check on payday? My first payday and I had no money! I was deflated. I had to forget about all the plans I had made for spending my coins. I was broke. Dreams of new shoes and movies and sweets simply vanished. Even though I'd never had any of those things, not being able to get them with my first check on my first payday felt like a loss. But…I had bus ticket, so I had a way home.

A month after my first day on the job, I received my first paycheck. I was so happy! While the check was not for a large amount of money, even by the standard of the day, I was proud to have earned it with my fish-smelling hands. With this paycheck I entered my life in the world of the working class.

Student Employment

I graduated high school and entered Sonoma State University. Going to school, studying, and playing basketball was not enough for me, so I got a job at the library. Working at the library was great because I got to study. I read all kinds of books, and I worked with different people.

The library job was my introduction to Bitter Bitches. My supervisor, a woman name Dale, was a sweet, kind, and pleasant supervisor. She was like everyone's grandmother, with a heart of gold. She had worked at the library for years. I mean *years.* Years and years and years.

This was a library, so it was quiet. There was no pressure to make sure the books were shelved or the card catalog updated. (Younger readers, a card catalogue was a paper version of the library search engine you use today. There was a paper card for each book, and you looked things up by title or subject. Seriously, young ones. We did this by hand.) There was only one exception to the pleasantness; it was named Gary.

Gary was my first BBP (Bitter Bitch with a Penis). Gary was Black, about five feet eight inches, slim, and he had long dreads. He was a professional student and had been at Sonoma State for eight years. He had a bachelor's degree and was working on his masters. Gary had been employed at the library for years. He was very laid-back. It was very clear he felt secure in his position.

Gary was not happy at the library. He was a student assistant, as I was, and he complained about the job every time I worked with him. The only time he wasn't complaining was when he was high. He was the only person I knew who could find a place to get high in the library. I was invited to join him but was always too scared to smoke weed in the library. His level of complaining was remarkable for someone who was so frequently stoned on the job.

Since Gary, I have encountered a number of Bitter Bitches with and without a penis. I have noticed that I encounter the most BBs in civil-service jobs. Civil-service jobs tend to give people a sense of job security. Employees function under the idea of "You can't fire me! My union will make sure I keep my job." I have found that only a few things will get a civil-service employee fired: 1) stealing money or property, 2) physical violence in the workplace, 3) job abandonment. If you are incarcerated and cannot make it to work for the next three or four years, you will be fired. Beyond these few things, it is nearly impossible to dislodge an entrenched civil servant. Honestly, you can come in and lose your bowels on your boss's desk, get a counseling memo, promise to go to Diarrhea Anonymous next week with the union's blessing, and you will keep your job.

Most jobs involve developing a routine. Many jobs are comprised of repetitive work that does not require much problem-solving or really any higher brain functions. While routine can provide stability, it can also lead to frequent mistakes and laziness. I think if you stay in one position for over three years and you have not perfected the work, you need to look for another type of work.

Most work in civil service tends to be routine. For example, mail comes in, you open the letter, you date-stamp the letter, you place the letter in a tray for pickup. Simple. That's it. If you do this eight hours a day, five days a week, boredom sets in. Before you know it, you get attacked by the bitterness bug. Bitter Bitch is a slow and progressive illness. One day you get an attitude about opening the letters and wonder why Ruby doesn't have to open letters. Then maybe the next day you get an attitude with Ruby, who used to be your lunch buddy, because she is not opening letters. Then you try to get others mad at Ruby. Before you know it, the bitterness has crept into the office and is slowly taking over the entire unit. Suddenly, everyone dislikes everyone.

One way to inoculate an office against the bitter bug is cross-training. When employees are encouraged to change their routines, it keeps them engaged in the work, stimulates the brain, and varies the people they interact with. Routines are boring. People look for distractions, and sometimes they are not positive for the workforce.

What has kept me from becoming a Bitter Bitch is frequently changing jobs. I have worked at many agencies and moved within agencies to keep myself interested in my work.

Food Service, 1970s Style

The library closed during summer break. I decide to get another job. I ended up taking three food-service jobs simultaneously: McDonalds, Jack-in the-Box, and the

Firehouse Cantina. I juggled three part-time positions and played basketball for three months. It was one of my worry-free summers. It was fun.

Although all three jobs were in the food-service industry, there were marked differences. McDonald's is basically a factory. You just show up, push buttons on the cash register, and put food on trays. The key to a McDonald's job is recognizing your two mandatory skills are smiling and being pleasant to customers. The most complex part of the job is making sure the Big Mac has two all-beef patties, special sauce, lettuce, cheese, pickles, onions on a sesame-seed bun. That's it. And in the seventies'70s, we all knew the jingle for quality assurance of a Big Mac.

I got the Firehouse Cantina job through my basketball coach. I learn how to make burritos, tacos, and other Mexican food. I enjoyed this job. My coworkers were my age, and we got along great and bonded unlike at any other job I can remember. We all liked and disliked the same customers. At the end of each shift, we would close the restaurant, turn up the music, clean, and have a great time.

This was one of my first exposures to hard- rock music. AC/DC's *Highway to Hell* entered my world consciousness, and I followed it deep into the world of hard rock. I had Funkadelic, Parliament, and Bootsy records, but they were not like AC/DC. Hard rock spoke to me in a way other music did not. Sharing this with my co-workers at the Cantina helped us bond.

Jack- in- the-Box was- —and still is- —my favorite fast- food restaurant. I like the freshness of their food and the greasy taste of the taco's. When I worked there, the lettuce, tomatoes, cheese, eggs, and ham were fresh. I can remember cooking omelet's on the grill in the early-morning hours when the restaurant was closed except for the drive-thru through. We would make all types of food at Jack's. It was an experiment with food every night or early morning hours. I enjoyed this job because I worked the overnight shift and, because I was the cook, really had no contact with customers because I was the cook. But there were some strange things happening at the Jack-in-the-Box drive-thru through.

We had nights we fought to keep up with drive-thru through demand. One night I dropped bread on the floor trying as I tried to get a burger out. I yelled to my supervisor, "What should I do? I dropped the burger!" She yelled, "Pick it up! Brush it off, and put it in a bag." I did just what she said. I wrapped the burger and keep the food moving. We were a team: management and line employees working together toward the same goal. .

> ***To this day I measure my drunkenness by how many tacos I order from Jack-in-the-Box.***

Jack-in-the-Box was not like McDonald's; it was so much better! Sure, it was fast food, but it was a fresh type of fast food. To this day I measure my drunkenness on by how many tacos I order from Jack's. Two tacos equal an average drinking night. Four tacos equals and "Oh no!! A night of drinking" Now, six tacos means I should be home in bed, because my breath as a passenger would make the driver drunk!

Working at Jack-in-the-Box was much better than McDonalds partly because we were a team of four. We all needed to pitch in to get the food out. McDonald's was different.

Families came to eat at McDonald's and would sit in the restaurant and enjoy their food. The work at McDonald's was quite different from Jack-in-the-Box. I was on a crew of ten. There was a person on fries, two people cooking burgers, two people dressing the burgers. Four people were cashiers and the cashier prepared the drinks. Then we had a cashier for the drive-through, and to watch us all we had a supervisor. At McDonald's there was no standing around if we had no customers; we had to clean the dining area, clean the bathrooms, and the counters. We had to clean and look busy constantly. This cleaning and looking busy led to animosity amongst the crew. There was always someone who did everything to avoid cleaning—especially the bathrooms. This person would talk, gossip, or just disappear into the back somewhere. This caused tension within the crew, because we all were aware of the crewmember who was avoiding the cleaning duties.

One reason the fast-food jobs were satisfying is that fast food produces a finished product right in front of you. In most office work, you rarely see a completed product. No matter how many envelopes you open, the next day there are still more envelopes to open. It never stops. Additionally, in fast food, customers say "Thank you" for their order. I was rarely thanked for stuffing envelopes at an office job.

This was college, and the jobs were great! I like to believe it was because I had no reason not to have a good time at work. I was not trying to save for a retirement plan. I had no kids, and if I did not like the boss, I could quit and find something else. I had no goals in life and I had no responsibility to anyone except myself.

Oregon

I soon relocated to Corvallis, Oregon, to attend Oregon State University. Yes another college.

My first year in Corvallis, I worked at a Meier & Frank department store during the Christmas season. It was called "Christmas" in the '80s. We had not widely adopted the term "holiday season." This was my first retail job—and my last. I learned really quickly that constantly folding clothes after people unfolded them was not for me. I would ask customers, "How can I help you?" but in my mind I was really thinking, "You can help your damn self!"

Retail is a hard job. Employees are Bitter Bitches without cubicles. People in retail positions need patience and understanding. It is hard to deal with people who wait until the last minute to shop and then wonder why the size they want is not in stock. Duh! We had it in stock last week, but you come in search of if it three days before Christmas, with your badass kids running through the store, and give me an attitude when you can't find what you want out on the floor. So, no, we don't have it. No, I don't have a secret stash in the back. No, I'm not looking for it. Yes, I got a little bitter.

I would go to the back and count to one hundred, then come back out and say, "I'm sorry, we don't have that size." I see now how bad that behavior was, but the constant interaction with rude people and the lack of positive interaction on the job led me to be defiant and bitter. I shop for Christmas far in advance now, because I don't want to be the target of a bitter retail employee!

I graduated from Oregon State University with a baby on the way. I learned quickly that a child makes you accountable for every decision. A child makes you get some goals. I had to get a real job that required my attendance daily. I couldn't quit simply because I was unhappy. I also realized that everybody has some type of boss to answer to, and sometimes the boss can make or break your day.

Descending into Hell: Civil Service

My first real job was at the Department of Motor Vehicles (DMV). Yes, what a way to start your work career after five years of college! In this job, I actually needed to report to work Monday through Friday and put on a happy face. This was my first real experience working with bitter people and bitter coworkers. The coworkers didn't faze me so much, because this was a job where people walked in the door mad at the DMV and mad at you just because you were behind the counter. Believe it or not, it is actually worse to work at the DMV than it is to visit it for your annual car-registration renewal. Patty and Selma Bouvier from the Simpson are real. I can testify to this.

When I started working at DMV, I was twenty-four, a young mother, and happy to have a job. I learned after accepting the job that the DMV was going through a change. They had initiated a telephone appointment system and were requiring appointments for all customers. Terrible idea! Customers had to phone in and make an appointment before they could be helped in the DMV field office. The DMV had four phone lines. As with so many government programs, the agency severely underestimated what the actual demand for services would be, and the DMV was not prepared for the volume of calls. And if you really want to piss off thousands of people, make a change to a system in which they have always been able to show up, wait six hours and get help to one where they show up and are told to go home, make an appointment, then come back and wait to be served. I am surprised no one got shot over this change.

The phone system was constantly lit up like a Christmas tree. The lights never went out. Trying to get through to the DMV was like trying to call a radio station to win free concert tickets—except instead of getting free passes to a great night, you got the joy of coming into the DMV to renew your license.

I transferred out of the DMV after a year. How lucky for me! I moved up in government agencies a small step and got a job at the Franchise Tax Board. I was called a tax clerk, but in actuality I was a professional file clerk in a large warehouse of paper tax returns. (Side note: The DMV was so bad that I found working for people who take everyone's money to be a better option with fewer BBs.) There were rows and rows of shelves with files containing many years of paper tax returns of the good people of California. My job was to file the returns. This was not a bad job until a time limit was implemented. When I realized I had to file quickly, I just filed. I would roll my cart down an aisle, pick a random spot, and shove the tax return in. I'm sure some tax returns were lost in the black hole of tax returns, never to be found again.

I lasted at this job about six months. There was no human contact except for breaks and lunch. This was job isolation at its finest.

I then moved on to the Department of Transportation, aka Caltrans. I worked in the mailroom with individuals I called the "Caltrans misfits." The mailroom at Caltrans was like the Island of Misfit Toys in the old *Rudolph* Christmas special. My supervisor was there because she had hurt her arms working as a toll collector on the bridge. (I surmise it came from flipping off too many people but could never confirm that.) There was another coworker who worked in the mailroom because he was blind in one eye. Another coworker had a prosthetic leg. There was another ready to retire, and basically he was just marking time. Another was there because of some type of adverse action that resulted in his demotion to the mailroom. I was there because I wanted out of the DMV, and sorting mail seemed far superior to anything I was currently doing.

We all worked together to manage the mail. We each took a floor and delivered mail in the morning and afternoon. There was not a lot to do but open envelopes, date-stamp letters, and deliver packages to offices. It was routine but as a temporary assignment did not appear to be awful.

I didn't have many goals at that point in life, but I knew finishing college with a degree and working in a mailroom was definitely not a goal on my life agenda.

Bitter Bitches continued to crop up throughout my jobs. They came in all shapes, sizes, genders, and career levels. Over the years, I learned to spot the BBs on the job, deal with them, avoid them, and inoculate myself against the BB virus. Not all of us are that lucky. Bitter Bitches are prolific and multiplying, and we must stop this trend.

We continue to build Bitter Bitches faster and faster as we eliminate opportunities for positive human contact.

Modernity and Bitter Bitches

The longer you are around, and the more you do something, the better you get at doing it. Unless, of course, you are a BB working for the State. I have developed a keen awareness of what creates BBs and where they flourish.

So why, with all the advances in modern technology and management, do we still have BBs? We continue to build Bitter Bitches faster and faster as we eliminate opportunities for positive human contact. Now we have self-checkout machines in grocery stores, retail stores, and banks. No longer do we have the opportunity to speak with an individual who can help with our simple transactions. Anything that is not problematic is handled by a touch screen and card reader.

A machine has no fresh ideas and doesn't care. Mr. Machine does not have to go home to an angry wife or demanding kids. He does not have to sit through human-resources lectures about safety and sexual harassment. He does not have to worry how he is going to pay his kids' tuition and medical costs. He does not have to save for retirement. Mr. Machine gets to help you with things that make you happy (giving you money, getting you through grocery stores faster, completing a price check).

We now expect that interacting with a machine is somehow faster and more convenient than with a person. We go out of our way to avoid positive human contact—opting to wait ten minutes in the self-checkout at the grocery store rather than seven minutes to interact with a clerk. We tell ourselves this is easier and faster. We are reducing our interactions with service people to times that we have a problem. This reality is spreading the Bitter Bitch virus.

The problem with this is we cannot solve basic problems that arise when using computers. If the ATM does not dispense the right amount of cash or the grocery scale does not register the correct weight of your bananas, you then have to seek out human help. You seek out customer service when you are angry and frustrated. Yelling at the machines is less satisfying than yelling at Jeff in customer service, so Jeff takes the brunt of your frustration.

The problem with this new system is that Jeff the grocery clerk used to see all customers. When he would ring most customers through, they'd thank him and say, "Have a great day!" When he got the occasional problematic customer, the negative "Fix this, you idiot!" was balanced by ten "Thanks!" Now, poor Jeff gets ten "Fix this stupid thing!" to everyone "Thanks!" Sometimes, one person can ruin your whole day—and fifteen angry people can really mess it up. Facing this negativity day in and day out without balance creates bitterness more and more quickly. Our need for convenience and our false sense of autonomy has created a world where the Bitter Bitch virus spreads likes mono at a college party.

There are plenty of ways to inoculate against and fight the BB virus. Chapter three provides many options. Read on, dear reader!

**AIN'T
NOBODY
GOT
TIME
FOR THAT!**

Chapter 3: Bossholes

I have never held the position or title of supervisor and

really never wanted to. I felt as though I had enough on my

plate supervising my two kids; I knew I didn't want to go to

work and be a mother there also. Yes, supervising is just

like mothering. I always wanted to just do my job and go

home at five as so many of us nine-to-five workers do. I

didn't realize until later that work became my life, and I should have worked to live and not lived to work.

I can only salute the people who love the supervisory role in life. There are great ones, and then there are some who just take the role too far. I'm sure we've have all had one of those in our years of employment. If you have not yet experienced one of these "A"-type supervisors, you eventually will.

In school I had good teachers and teachers who didn't give a shi$t. Similarly, I've had many supervisors with the same differing philosophies in my years of working. Some supervisors would take their time to show you the proper way to complete your work, and other supervisors would criticize you, and then show you how to do the work. I guess this technique helped them feel stronger, because they had the power or answers you are in search of. Both have their own way of getting the job done. I like to think that giving some encouragement helps with teaching a new job, but as I said in the beginning, I have never been a supervisor.

It takes work and patience to become a great supervisor, because it is a position that also requires respect. If you can gain the respect of your coworkers, you can get almost anything you need done. People who have no respect for the people they work with have no desire or commitment to do things for you. You can ask and plead, but the employees' drive to get it done is zero, because basically they do not like you.

When I worked for the State of California, I had all types of supervisors who had the title mainly because they passed a test and were next on the list to get promoted. They did not get the job because of their skills; they got it because of their ability to pass a test. This did not include how well they are liked. I've had many supervisors who were just stupid. There is no other way to explain it. They never had any people skills. They became used to talking to rocks on a daily basis, and that is what their personality turned out to be: a rock.

Dealing with "rock" personality supervisors is one of the hardest things to do, mainly because they will not share any advice you need to complete your job.

The DMV was where I started working for Bossholes— defined as a boss that is an a$$hole. This makes me think DMV is the bosshole farm: you start out as an employee, a little sprout, and grow into a big-ass uncontrollable weed that can't be killed.

Grover was my first supervisor at the DMV in 1985. Grover was about five feet two and two hundred pounds. He wore all his khaki pants about an inch below his chest, with a white shirt tucked in and a white pocket protector to complement his outfit. He wore a leather belt to keep his pants in place and completed his wardrobe with black shoes and black socks to match. Grover was shaped like a washing-machine box with glasses. He looked like Deputy Dog from the cartoons.

Grover had been at the DMV field office for years. He talked as if the building had been built around him. He had over thirty years of state service, and he was proud of it. He wore his DMV supervisor badge with honor.

Grover shared with me his many years of experience working as a DMV employee. When he talked about employees and customers, he always presented each in a good light. I knew this couldn't be true, because I was twenty-four and everybody talked about the DMV as a hellhole to work in. Listening to Grover made me think, "Oh, maybe this won't be so bad." He used his supervisor skills to smooth a new employee like me into thinking I just landed a great job with customer who would be happy to see me. Oh, how wrong could I ever be?

I can remember the customer from hell. This customer had seen about 6 different motor vehicles clerks. Everyone knew him, so when it became his turn in line, there was a rush for the bathroom, water and break time, anything but to take him as the next customer.

One morning I had no choice but to call him next. I knew this was going to be a challenge. I had faith in my DMV knowledge and I thought I could handle the customer from hell. He stepped up to my window with his stack of papers that clearly show evidence of the six clerks he had seen prior to me. Once I sorted through all of the papers I realized I was missing the one important paper, which was the title to the car. I tried to explain to him (in my most nice calm work voice) "that the title would be need before I could complete anything with this car". He proceeded to explain to me that the title was there and I need to look again at the papers he just gave me. This conversation replayed for about ten minutes. The frustration began to creep in to my work voice, as I explain again "if you can find the title in these papers then show it to me". Soon the conversation exceeded the volume for DMV office work and Grove slowly approached and asked could he help. I said sure and tried to explain the problem. I soon had the urge to go to the bathroom and sit until Captain DMV aka Grover saved the day.

Biggie Small and Tupac were the names I gave to the last supervisors I had at DMV. Biggie Small was a lady who weighed about 290 pounds and was approximately five foot seven. She was the type to rush into the office to check to see if you made it to work on time. It did not matter that her scheduled time to be at work was 8:30. She would arrive at seven to check on you. She would come to work with the plan that she would just do some knitting until her shift started.

Tupac was the boss of Biggie Small she was ready to retire in five years so she would slip into the office wearing shades, even if it was raining. She was about 125 pounds 5 feet 5 inches she was cool beyond belief. She would email her instructions from her office for the day to us and we would all wonder when she arrived at the office. Well we were wondering she would slip out the office. She was in management all that was required from her was to complete four hours in the office each day in order to claim an 8 hour day of work. So that is what she would do. It was like now you see her know you don't.

Dale at the library was my first real supervisor. I was 17. She was so sweet and nice but old and naive.

Firehouse Cantina Tina was cool. She was just a few years older than me and the perfect boss to have when you are eighteen. She got high and drank beer, a great combination that matters when you're young.

I would like to start off with one of the best supervisors. That was my boss when I worked with the county, "someone I'll call" Nichole. She was one of the best supervisors I worked for and was always a fair lady in the work world. She never judged people on their gender, race, or religion and was always a mediator when problems occurred. She was the finest.

Nichole was a supervisor who greeted everyone with a smile and a "Good morning." She did this on a daily basis. This was one of the little things made her special. I would watch her handle problems within the unit, never losing her patience or temper, always being even-handed.

Connie the Crackhead

As I mentioned earlier, my first full-time job after college was with the State of California. I descended straight into hell and took a job at the DMV. To this day I still wonder why I took that job.

When you start a new job, there are a few things you need to do, like distinguishing the good employees from the bitter employees. I learned this quickly. The DMV was a hot zone. Men would come in and flirt with the clerks to get their registration fixed or to get a temporary permit to drive their car for the next year. They did whatever they could to work their way through the DMV system of hell. I found out much later that the DMV could be a lucrative side hustle. This was in the '80s, and the world of paperwork was still alive and well; you could be creative with a date stamp or a time clock that you had the key for.

What I didn't learn until later was that some of the employees were functioning crackheads. They would smoke at night and show up in the morning for work. I was naive to the world of crack and really gullible to the crackheads. I thought since they had a job, they must have been all right. Sure, you need me to loan you a few extra dollars to pay your rent because someone broke into your car again and stole your wallet with all your money in it because you just cashed your paycheck and we just got paid—no problem; I understand. Oh, your eyes are red because you've been crying. I understand. How much money do you need?

Bottom line: figure out who are the working crackheads on the job. These are people who are employed but spend their nights in the crack house. The easiest way to identify these employees is to take a look at who is at work the day after payday. And if payday is on a Friday, you can include the drinking crackheads also, because they won't be at work on Monday either.

I was new, and pretty young, and naïve, and unaware—and let's add stupid. I thought people who came to work didn't do drugs, so I guess I was an easy mark for the working supervisor who I found out later was a crackhead. Yes, and this was the time when people were really doing crack. They got paid on the first of the month, and I got paid around the tenth. Connie, my supervisor, was well aware when my paycheck arrived. She had already smoked her own paycheck, so she would show up for work with red eyes, claiming she was sick. I believed her, so when she would ask me to borrow $300, I would say, "No problem." I knew she had a job, and maybe she was sick; I just didn't know what from. She was pretty thin, but I thought she just worked out. I loaned her the $300 and didn't see her for the next three days; she called in sick. Wow, she must really be sick. I had no idea until a fellow employee told me,

"Connie's not sick. She's doing that thing." "What thing?" Soon I realized what "that thing" was.

Office gossip soon spread: she had borrowed money from everyone in office. And since I was the new employee, I was unaware, and who is going to talk about the boss. She was a person one should look up to. She was supposed to represent authority. Someone you should respect. Someone with knowledge. Someone who was above me in the work hierarchy. Little did I know she might have had knowledge of the job, but she lacked knowledge of life.

Connie was only a few years older than me, but this was when I realized age doesn't matter; experience and etiquette play a vital role in supervising individuals.

I ran into Connie about ten years later, after I had left the DMV and moved up the chain in state service. For some reason, she assumed I must be in the same position. That's when I realized she had no respect for my knowledge, and I had none for hers. She had a drug problem and had abandoned her job several times. That's the strange thing with state service. You cannot show up for work and just apologize with some strange excuse like "I couldn't find my car for four days." Lady, it was at the crack house; you just needed to look out the window. You'll be sent to the Employee Assistance Program (EAP), and they will forgive you, and you can have your job back. Sad but true. If they would just fire some of these people, maybe you could get good service at the DMV.

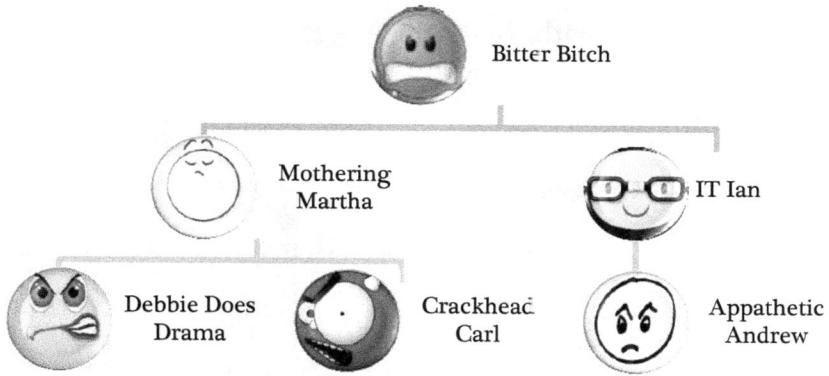

Bitter Bitch

Mothering Martha

IT Ian

Debbie Does Drama

Crackhead Carl

Appathetic Andrew

Chapter 4: Bitchology

*B*itter Bitches come in all shapes and sizes—in all poorly,

inappropriately dressed shapes and sizes. Each BB flavor

brings something unique to the stress in the office. Some

are passive-aggressive. Some kick up drama just for fun.

Some love to throw you under the bus. Learning to identify

the flavor of BB you are dealing with will make the daily

drudgery of sharing the same industrial-carpeted, overly cooled space with them more bearable.

Each BB type requires a unique set of coping skills. Bitter colleagues present pitfalls at work. Not only do you risk contracting the BB virus yourself, many of these BBs can cause you real and significant problems at work. Unlike diffusing a movie bomb, not all BBs have the same trigger wire.

Mothering Martha

Aw, Martha. We all know Martha. We all hate the fact that office birthday-party celebrations exist because Martha insists on them.

Martha is the office organizer. She does the birthday club, the holiday potlucks, and the water club. She is forever passing around some card and a donation request for someone's birthday/baby shower/recent loss/illness or other thing that you really don't care about or want to donate five dollars to. She likes to be in charge of small office events but would never seek a managerial position.

Martha loves the good ol' days, even when she has only been at the agency for two years. She will quickly let employees know how things were done in the past. Martha believes that whatever procedures were in place when she was hired constitute the only way things should be done. She does not believe in evolution—at least of policies and procedures.

Martha has an unmatched and unjustified level of self-confidence. She is not afraid of voicing her opinion or exercising her suggestion of how things should be completed. She will happily advise you of what is appropriate to wear in the office, suggesting that ill-fitting "below-the-knee" skirts from Target and a "nice sweater, perhaps with a cat pin" would be a good addition to your professional rotation.

Martha loves her crafts. She finds ways to incorporate them into her "duties not otherwise specified." She invites you to join her for a weekend scrapbooking club and gives you her extra coupons to craft stores. She carries at least three bags into the office, the largest dedicated to crafting supplies she breaks it out every moment she has in the break room.

Martha is very "Christian" in her approach to the job. She loves the job but hates everyone there. Despite her general disapproval of change and other employees, she never seeks advancement—because that would constitute change.

She is rooted in her cubicle. Changing offices would prove more traumatic to her than moving Fichus (which she probably has in her office). She has pictures of all her pets, family, and friends posted throughout her cubicle. She only adds photos, never removes them. For older Marthas, you can see their children grow from birth though school to marriage and family by looking around her cube. For single Marthas, you see their cats multiply to dangerous levels for any single woman.

While Martha hates change, somehow her personal dress code has evolved. She used to dress professionally for work. Over time, as she became comfortable in the office, her clothes started to reflect that. There is an unstated fear that the year before retirement, she will be rocking a Snuggie at work.

Martha's personal change in dress code does not change her opinion about how others should dress in the office. She gives copious and unrequested advice to young women about the benefits of taupe pantyhose, knee-length skirts, and practical (read UGLY) heels. She doles out this advice while wearing a floor-length khaki skirt and sweater with a cat on it.

While Martha is annoying, she is useful. She has institutional knowledge. She actually has useful answers to questions. She enjoys being a resource. If she doesn't have the answers, she knows where to get them.

The problem with Martha is she understands that her information and knowledge give her power and job security. She guards the answers like a leprechaun guarding his pot of gold. The only thing Martha wants more than her gold is deference. You earn your one piece of gold by bowing to her superior knowledge. It requires ass-kissing her khaki-clad hindquarters.

And, like the leprechaun, she has a drawer full of shamrocks and rainbows to decorate her cube every March.

Crackhead Connie

While my own personal Connie came in the form of a supervisor at the DMV, Connies exist at all levels of the work world. That was my first horrible discovery. I thought people with addiction issues would be confined to lower-level job categories, but I was mistaken.

Coworkers with addiction issues lend a unique flavor of drama to the workplace. They have a legitimate problem that they need help with. Most need some level of professional help. Their drama revolves around money and time.

Connies will gamble away their rent or drink away their Eectric bill payment and then be in dire straits and ask you for help. They draw you in by making you feel like you are a good person for helping out someone in need.

The first time they request money, you listen to their story. They are short on rent. If they don't pay rent, they will be evicted. They only need a couple hundred until next payday and will hit you back.

Reluctantly, you give them a couple of hundred dollars but make yourself feel better by telling yourself you did a good deed. Then payday rolls around. They can't pay you the full amount they owe you but have a good excuse. The repayment dribbles back in over months, if at all.

Then, before they have repaid you for their first loan, they need money for another emergency and ask you for fifty dollars. The excuse seems legitimate, but you still are owed for their rent three months ago. If you get drawn into this loop, you will soon be helping another person whose only relationship to you is that you share a break room. Suddenly, you're supporting another adult.

Connies are confusing because, often, you can't figure out why they have so many money issues. You know their job class. You know about their kids and commitments because they tell you all about them when asking for money. The numbers don't add up to a need to borrow all the time.

If you don't lend money, the Connie will let you know how bad her life is and use it as a reason for not showing up to her job or not getting her work done. She hides her addiction and tries to cite you as the reason she is doing poorly on the job and in life.

The thing is, you are not responsible in any way for paying Connie's debts. The trick is staying out of this drama in the first place. A strict policy of not lending coworkers money is the easiest defense. But, if you give in once, you need to cut it off after that. Otherwise, it becomes a vicious loop.

Debbie Does Drama

Every office has an office drama queen. Everyone in the office wonders how she got hired and when she's going to be fired. Everyone hopes the boss will wise up and just get rid of her.

This is the employee who is late at least twice a week. The only thing more certain than Debbie rolling in late is that she will always have excuses.

Debbie never has a simple excuse. She never just overslept. No, with Debbie, the car wouldn't start (and her car appears to be *very* unreliable); the baby ate her keys; she was walking into the office and got stopped by the news to do a "person on the street" interview about pet adoption, and on the spot she adopted this cute chinchilla and just had to give them an interview about it.

Debbie loves to talk. The sound of her own voice drives lengthy explanations about the reasons she is frequently late. When she doesn't have herself to talk about, she likes to gossip. This type of employee knows all the office gossip mainly because she is often the subject of it.

Debbie hunts for gossip. Every day she moves from cubicle to cubicle asking questions or talking about her weekend plans, even though it's Tuesday. Debbie the drama queen always has something to talk about except the main reason everyone is there, and that's work.

Debbie appears to the complete stranger or new employee as a sweet and caring coworker. She appears sweet and innocent only because the new employee is unaware of the office danger Debbie poses. The drama queen is like a panda. You see it and think, "Aw…how cute!" right before you get too close and it eats you.

She continually needs fresh meat: an unbiased party to be on her side of the argument. Someone who, when she complains about not getting her break at the scheduled time, will believe that management is in the wrong. The new prey does not know that this is the third time this month that the drama queen arrived at the office only thirty minutes before her schedule break because there was an accident on the freeway, and the person involved in the accident was her mother's friend-from-work cousin on her remarried father's side. Yes, that's what I said. Let me repeat it. She was late because there was an accident on the freeway, and the person involved in the accident was her mother's friend from work's cousin on her remarried father's side.

Sick leave and vacation are only words on Debbie's time sheet. She is an earn-and-burn type of employee. Like the guy in *Office Space,* Debbie comes in, finds a dozen ways to kill time, but always manages to look busy.

Debbie manages to spend a lot of time on her cell phone. It's hard to tell if it's work related or if she's talking to her husband, babysitter, boyfriend, kids, or neighbor—or placing a lunch order or getting a payday loan. Most people wouldn't care about this except for the fact that Debbie likes to make the calls from the bathroom and tie up the one decent stall for forty minutes at a time.

After years at work, a Debbie sometimes morphs into a mothering Martha without ever leaving her same cubicle. Debbie has to evolve to keep her job. Once the evolution is complete, however, she remains stuck for the remainder of her career.

IT Ian

IT Ians have a deep belief that they are smarter and cooler than everyone else in the office. They also find themselves hilarious. The thing is Ians are not smarter, cooler, or funnier than anyone else. They are just more condescending and awkward.

IT Ian's favorite complaint is how overworked he is and how dumb everyone else is. Don't know how to write the code to make your new software interface with the company server? You are an idiot! Can't figure out the fourteen-step process to log onto the LAN from home? How dumb can you be?! And what do you mean you don't have a twenty-sided die in your desk to help you make decisions? However do you function?

Ians have a mark; it is inappropriate office wear. Left to their own devices, Ians will don shirts sporting logos of their favorite video games, sci-fi characters, or anything anime. If there is an assigned uniform, they will add stickers, pins, or other such ephemera to their ID badge to indicate their uniqueness.

Ian makes getting things fixed difficult. You dread calling him because of his condescending attitude, accompanied by a continuous monologue, while he tries to fix your monitor, about how overworked he is. This leads other office staff to put off taking care of small issues, ultimately leading to much larger issues in the long run.

Ians are also more likely to cross lines. Their awkwardness regularly manifests as sexual harassment and racially insensitive remarks. IT Ian will find it amusing to comment about how much Bev in Accounting looks like some fantasy girl from an anime show, and he will casually suggest that she wear tiny skirts and put her hair in pigtails so she can cosplay at work. He regularly skirts the line of office decorum—but never enough to get him fired.

Ians are hard to discipline. Even when a supervisor calls Ian in to discuss his behavior or dress, Ian will later dismiss the conversation because his "boss is stupid" or "doesn't understand how important World of Warcraft" is in helping him develop teamwork skills.

Subtlety does not work with Ian. He requires direct and blunt communication. This again is hard in an office where politeness and decorum are valued. However, Ians will persist in bad behavior until called out loudly and bluntly to "Please stop it with the conversation about your Brony convention this weekend. I don't care how awesome it was to dress up as a pink pony and chill with your bros."

Apathetic Andrew

Everyone knows an Apathetic Andrew. Everyone hates Apathetic Andrew. Andrew makes getting help at customer service infuriatingly difficult. The only thing worse than having to work with Andrew as a customer is working with Andrew as a colleague.

Andrew has decided that he really doesn't care enough to do a good job. His sole goal in life seems to be to do just one more thing than necessary to keep from getting fired.

While Andrew doesn't seem to care about his job, he definitely cares about the rules. He knows exactly how many times he can clock in late in a quarter without getting penalized. He knows how many minutes late he can come back from lunch without getting written up. He knows how many phone calls can go unreturned before someone alerts his boss that he is slacking. He knows all of this because he routinely pushes the limits of doing nothing on the job.

Apathetic Andrews are dangerous. They annoy you, and you get tired of covering for their lazy butt, so you begin to play dangerous games of chicken.

If you and Andrew split the job of answering a phone, his apathy and unwillingness to work makes you resentful. One day, the phone starts to ring. You are tired of covering for Andrew, so you let the phone ring. Andrew lets the phone ring. You both sit, not acknowledging each other but silently willing the other person to *answer the damned phone!*

The problem with this is that having an apathy contest with Andrew is like having a staring contest with a cat. He will always either win or walk away and show you his butt.

Apathetic Andrew is the most dangerous of the BBs. His lack of initiative and unwillingness to do anything until pushed makes other employees resentful. As the resentment of Andrew spreads in the office, work slows down and bad behaviors develop.

Unfortunately, firing Andrew is hard. He knows just how far he can push, and then he kicks into work mode and pulls himself back from the brink of being fired. Controlling the rapid spread of the BB virus in an Andrew-infested office takes a lot of work on the supervisor's part. Setting weekly goals for Andrew and doing things like desk audits can help change some of the bad behavior. Ultimately however, the best solution is for a supervisor to help Andrew understand he needs to find work elsewhere.

Elevating Eva

In well-functioning offices there sits an unpretentious employee: Elevating Eva. Eva arrives to work early, prepared for her day. Her dress is professional, and she walks into the office with a smile, greeting her coworkers with an unironic "Good morning." She possesses a positive attitude and understands what need to be done to accomplish her daily work duties. Eva actively repels the BB virus.

Elevating Eva is not a true BB. She never really gets infected with the BB virus. She still hates her job most of the time but fights the need to bring others into her misery about going to work.

Elevating Eva brings hope, not troll dolls, into the office. She carries a glow that employees admire. She conveys happiness. She may not be thrilled about being on the job, but she has discovered how to be a professional and not display her unhappiness on her face. Eva will acquire the skills of her current position and be promoted to a new position. This movement prevents her from becoming infected with the BB drama within her office. This type of person is on a career mission to the top and will never stay in any position long.

Eva avoids the office drama. She will acknowledge it but will not engage in the conversation. She manages to redirect the topic to something more positive within the workplace. She is pleasant when she needs to be, without being a kiss-up. Her pleasantries appear to be genuine, and she is not a brownnoser. Eva has the ability to complete her assignments and a little office small talk also. Eva has learned to rise above the office bitterness, which has her moving up the career ladder swiftly.

Eva makes friends within the office. She treats each employee as a coworker, and that's it. She rarely engages in after-work drinks. She has a life outside the office. This confounds the Bitter Bitches she encounters. She tries to keep her work life and home life separate.

Eva is a breath of fresh air. The office plants appreciate this.

Bitter Bitches Be Gone!

Bitter Bitches are tiresome to deal with and can be dangerous to your career. Much like identifying poisonous and helpful plants in the woods before you camp, it is helpful to understand the poisonous versus helpful employees at work. You can deal with and disarm the BBs, but only if you can identify them first!

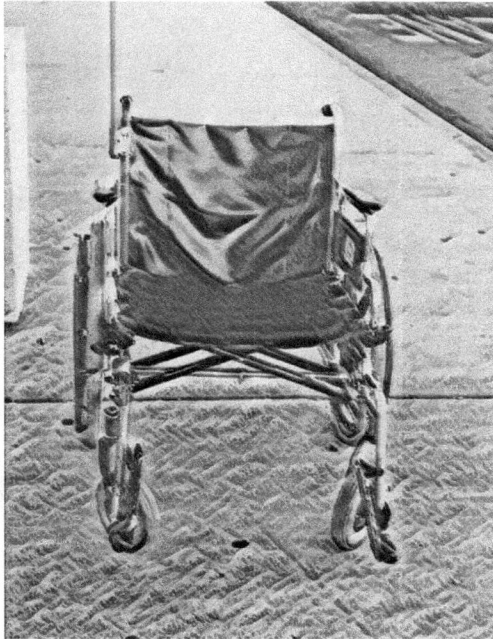

Chapter 5: Disability: When the J-O-B Is G-O-N-E

*T*he hardest thing about getting sick at work,

legitimately ill, is that no one believes you. Some

of us have the privilege of having sick days (and this *is* a privilege in the United States), but we all know people who cash in on them when they just don't want to come into the office. Lots of people fake a cough on a call with the boss. Those of us who have done this more than once learn it is better to fake a GI issue, because nobody—and I mean nobody—wants to hear about your diarrhea.

When you get ill everyone thinks you are faking it. Depending on the illness, you may not want to reveal it to your employer. Something like needing a hip replacement is seen as an acceptable reason to ask for extended sick leave. However, things like soft-tissue damage or carpal tunnel syndrome are seen as make-believe diseases. If your illness comes with a stigma, (*e.g.*, a mental health diagnosis, AIDS) you may not ever want to reveal the nature of your illness to your employer. Your illness is not seen as a legitimate reason to miss work, and even worse, you still are in a ton of pain.

As a result, employees learn to use different excuses. I will not be in today because:

- I am not feeling well.
- My kid is sick.
- My car would not start.
- Public transportation is not running this morning.
- My mother needs my help.
- The power at my house is not working.
- I need to go take care of personal business.
- I did not sleep well last night.
- My cat is stuck in a tree.
- My dog is sick.

- I'm waiting on the cable man

Sometimes these excuses are legitimate. There are times when your mother will really need your help for the day. Some days you need a mental-health day (something we do not see as legitimate in the United States). Sometimes you know that if you have to see that little rat subhuman of a boss you will snap and try stabbing people with a plastic spork so you call in sick. But people use these excuses so often to cover up, just ditching work, that employers no longer see them as legitimate excuses.

Becoming Disabled

Most disabilities that prevent people from working full time do not develop in a single day. Occasionally people get in an accident that clearly makes them disabled for the job. You work on a construction site and there is an accident where you crush your arm and it has to be amputated. That is a clear-cut case of becoming disabled in the construction trade.

At least you might think so.

The more I try and work with Disability Insurance, the more capricious they appear to be. Take the construction worker with the amputated arm. By all reasonable understanding, the worker has lost a primary bodily function necessary for performing their job.

Disability Insurance has a well-known practice that they reject more than 99 percent of all claims on the first attempt. This has nothing to do with a large number of illegitimate claims being submitted. Instead, it is a bureaucratic trick to frustrate people and get them to stop asking for benefits. Bureaucracies bank on you getting frustrated with an overwhelming amount of stupidity and opting to walk away. This creates the sad state where you have to tap deep into your inner Bitter Bitch to even make a dent in getting what you have earned and now need.

I spent 25 years trying not to become a BB. Now, the federal government is forcing me to become one in order to survive.

Back to that construction worker. After he was rejected the first time because he dared to ask for benefits he earned, he has to go to trial. The morning of the trial maybe the Judge on his way into the job at the court house got stuck in construction zone traffic jam and he has suddenly transformed into a Bitter Bitch with a Penis today. He spends the twenty minutes in stop-and-go traffic fuming about how "stupid construction workers are preventing me from doing MY VERY IMPORTANT JOB!" When he reaches the hearing of the construction worker, his hemorrhoids are still aggravated from the extra time in traffic. As a result, he rules "Just because you lost one arm does not make you eligible for disability. You can become a construction greeter (not a real job in construction, but reality of the work world rarely intervenes in Disability Insurance decisions). You can answer phones on the construction site. You can hold the stop sign at the end of the road, so I would not have been stuck in a traffic jam."

Never take for granted that your disability is going to be approved. The folks deciding disability claims have no medical training. They have never been seriously ill at any point in their life. They are paid to use stupidity and errors to frustrate people who are seriously ill. It is the perfect job for a very lazy sadist.

Unlike our theoretical construction worker, most people see their disability come on more slowly. There is a period when you just don't feel well and begin needing to take frequent sick days. Then you have to go out on temporary disability to try and fix the issue. It is partially fixed. Then you return. Then you aggravate the issue and have to go out again. Eventually, reluctantly, you accept that you will not be able to work full time anymore. That's when you have to file for disability.

As much as you might hate your job, you discover your desire to work as it is taken away. Many of us want to contribute to the world in some form. For most of us, our work, no matter how mundane, is part of that contribution. We define ourselves by our jobs to some extent. Losing the ability to work a regular job is surprisingly disheartening. Fighting to work at a job you hate is one of the big paradoxes of becoming disabled.

The minute you submit your disability claim you are labeled a scammer, a criminal, lazy and a liar in the eyes of the Disability folks. It does not matter that you have worked full time for the past twenty-five years and you have paid into Social Security. No one who has ever worked on processing disability claims has ever, even for a second, believed the initial claim is legitimate. I am pretty sure any employee of Disability Insurance who reviews a claim and says, "This sounds legitimate," must be tazered and demoted to the mail room to rethink their reckless behavior. You could submit photos of your mangled body, testimony from a dozen doctors, and your actual severed limb, and the disability office would send a letter saying, "We need more evidence."

The only way Social Security labels you disabled is if you have a deadly illness and can barely function. The doctors have to write you a prescription for a coffin before the disability office thinks, "Well maybe she might be in a bit of pain."

The process of filing for disability is a demeaning experience. Strangers who have yelled at you and treated you like you are a criminal and the scum of the earth then demand detailed medical records. They sit you in a room with other strangers and ask you to detail bodily processes and functions. They question you about why you did not do this process or that process that you never heard of but should have somehow spontaneously gained knowledge of when you got sick.

It is immensely frustrating to have spent months or years trying to work while sick, paying into disability, doing everything you can to keep your job, and then be called a slacker and a leech. Never mind that you are only asking for what you have paid in to Social Security your entire career.

The most disheartening part of this whole process is you are forced to beg for $800 a week in disability from someone who has repeatedly demonstrated they have no ability to actually process a claim and still draw a full salary and benefits.

Trying to Work

It took months for me to accept that I could no longer work. I had a great job. This was the first time in my life I was making good money at a great job. It was worth getting up early every day, which I did—and I have never been a morning person.

It was in November 2011 when my back decided it had had enough.

Initially, I did not know what was wrong I just knew I had terrible pain and could not walk. After days and multiple visits to Kaiser- multiple visits for a single issue is normal for Kaiser- the doctor finally ordered an MRI. At that point, he realized I had a bulging disc that was pushing on a nerve that operated my leg. I was in terrible pain, and my leg had been hurting a long time. The old song "Your leg bone is connected to your backbone" is really true!

That day, I had to be taken to the emergency room. The hospital staff realized I was in serious pain. They admitted me immediately and hooked up the IV painkillers.

Oh, the drugs! The morphine killed the pain, but it also killed any logical thinking. My brain took a nice vacation to a neon-colored beach, while my body remained in the ER.

It was only after my brain boarded a flight for the lovely shores of Morphine Bay that the doctor came in to speak with me. The doctor could have told me anything, and I would have agreed. I really did not care about a single thing at this point. He could have been a graduate of the University of Phoenix in English lit and I would've been like, "Okey-dokey! Cut away, artichokey!"

Honestly, I think the decision to ask patients to make critical decisions only after they are high on painkillers seems a bit questionable. It is like asking your friend to pay your bar bill after he is nine drinks into the night. I think this is how medical groups get people to pay for that expensive $75.00 aspirin. You only know about it when you see the medical care bill months later.

Post-Surgery: Part I

The surgery went according to the doctor's plan. I lost some functionality, and running is no longer in my future. The pain subsided a bit, but I still have a long recovery.

During recovery, my doctors kept me on minimal amounts of painkillers. The medication kept the pain at a low hum, but never completely eliminated it.

I feared addiction to painkillers. The last thing I wanted to do was trade back and leg pain for an addiction. I tried to take the pain like a champ but soon realized I needed those painkillers. I was unable to stand, drive, or cook for myself. As someone who had been a functioning, self-sufficient adult, not being able to care for myself was a terrible feeling. I was at the mercy of other people. This was their time to repay me if I had every exercised the attitude of a BB. At my age yes, it was the "big pay back, revenge" for some people.

After months, I gained some functionality, and the pain was at a dull roar instead of a constant scream. I have yet to regain full function of my body. Five years, four surgeries, and numerous attempts at physical therapy and rehabilitation later, I am still not back to my baseline before I got hurt.

I try to keep up the positive, but this was one of my "come to Jesus" moments: I realized my body is old and needs to rest. I can still function in bursts, but I no longer bounce back the way I did when I was 25. I can still party like a rock star, but I recover like a grandmother. More like a grandmother of six. Maybe twelve. It depends on the day.

Applying for Disability

I could no longer work at my old position. I was in too much pain and lacked the physical capacity to work and compete at the fast pace job. This was devastating. I was a self-sufficient adult with two children at home, enjoying my life, and my capacity to be independent was stripped from me.

I think I am a competent and intelligent woman. I have worked for the government for years. Even with this, I found the process of trying to apply for disability confusing, frustrating, and degrading. Confusion, opacity, and inconsistency are added to the process to dissuade people from accessing benefits they deserve. It is purposely so confusing that people who are in pain and not at one hundred percent physically and mentally will simply give up and go away.

I had worked my entire adult life, and at age fifty, when I was making the most money of my career, my back went out. I applied for disability and was turned down. I challenged the decision and was turned down again. And again. And again. My claim has been rejected a total of six times to date, and the fight continues.

The first time I challenged my rejected claim, I was seen by a judge with an approval rating of 17 percent. I had a better chance of him making a free throw from center court than have him approve my disability. This man sat on the bench looking like Jabba the Hutt and judged me. He had no interest in hearing my rebuttal. His decision was written on his face when I walked in the door.

His questions were aimed at proving I was still capable of occasionally using my limbs with the assumption that me being upright indicated I was capable of working a forty-hour week. He asked me questions like, "Who picks up your glasses if you drop them?" I wanted to reply that if I can see them, I pick them up, duh! I was not saying I was totally handicapped and completely unable to work. The line of questioning was clearly meant to humiliate me and make me feel that if I could microwave a breakfast sandwich, I should be able to do construction work full time.

Surgery II

Unable to work and still in pain, I faced another surgery. My second major surgery came approximately four years later. This time the surgeon went through the front of my neck. The pain I experienced was terrible when I awoke from the surgery. It felt as though my throat was on fire. I screamed and cried and asked for painkillers. I was assured that I only needed to push the button and the painkillers would magically drip into my IV.

It took time to get the pain under control. This is not to say the pain was gone. It was simply reduced to the equivalent of background noise, not a screaming siren.

I was not surprised I could not get adequate pain control. Doctors have been taught that everyone in pain is faking it and really just seeking drugs. Additionally, I am a black woman. Doctors think all women—especially black women—overstate their pain and really just want to be addicted to drugs. I have never wanted to kick a doctor in the private, tender areas more than when I was trying to get help for pain. I mean, I delivered two babies! I am guessing the most pain any of my doctors had felt was a cavity or stepping on a Lego. Lego my painkillers is what they needed to do.

Moving Forward

I would not have chosen to leave work at fifty. I did not want to leave work and sought solutions to allow me to continue working. Only when those failed did I seek disability.

While I was forced to leave my work, I still learned from the experience. We need to learn our limitations. Sometimes we take a break in life, but most of the time we push forward. I am still the one who provides for my household financially.

It was not as if I was magically granted an additional provider when I became disabled. My kids and I still need to eat. We still need housing. I still want them to be able to go to college, and come home to do their laundry, and come see Mom. I paid into disability on the off chance something would go awry before I had enough in the bank to retire and live out my days. Now, I am fighting for a small stipend to help cover basic needs.

I am a mother and a provider. We as women learn there are no breaks. We do not have a chance to vote on who is going to go to work today. We learn to suck it up and go in while we're in pain or fighting through a fog of pain medications. All the while, we are told that our pain is not really that bad and we must be too sensitive and weak to know what real pain is like.

A few months after my second surgery, the pain had not abated. I could no longer take the pain. My brain would scream out in pain, and I would fight through it. I knew I had to work. Disney lied: mice do not mend clothing, and birds don't cook. You have to pick through the lentils yourself.

Disability is not a paid vacation. Disability can lead to a rabbit hole filled with depression. You sit home, and suddenly you realize you no longer have much contact with the world. You talk to the television. You try to guess the prices on the game shows, and you tell yourself *Jeopardy!* will make you smarter, even though you miss every question.

You lose your social connections if you don't reach out to people. Without work, you have no built-in reason for social interaction.

You find the old adage is true: "Out of sight, out of mind." People forget about you. Facebook is not a substitute for real people. Facebook is like signing up for people's vacation pictures, status updates about kids and food, and overly happy posts about their amazing lives. And you—you realize you can't go anywhere because you have another doctor's appointment Tuesday. So you just hit "like" on your friends' vacation pictures with the hope that you might be able take a trip again someday, too.

A Little Light

Comedy allows me a little relief from the house. I go to open mics (shows at bars and other venues where anyone can get up and tell jokes for a few minutes) to practice my art. I talk to other comics and help them write new material. This forces me to get out of the house and have some contact with human people and stay social.

I was lucky to be involved in this comedy world prior to becoming disabled. I had connections outside the office. I had a passion and some social activities to engage in before my back failed me.

Additionally, if I am too ill, in too much pain to leave the house, I can skip a mic. I can stay in, take care of my health, and look forward to the next time I can go out and work on my craft.

If you are reading this now and work is your life, your friends are at work, and your social life revolves around the office, you need to seek out some other passion, stat. There is no guarantee you will be able to work the rest of your life. You may be fired. You may lose your capacity to work. Your company may close. Having a passion and friends outside the office provides a lifeline. It has proven to be critical to keeping me sane and moving forward through this journey.

Today, as I listen to my girlfriends every day and they talk about the bitter bitches they work with and the bitter bitch customers I think peanut butter and jelly sandwiches are not that bad.

Sometimes you might miss your co-workers as I did but once I see their faces and they began to remind (talk) about the job and the BBP's, I realize being at home is not that bad. The pay is much lower but I only have to listen to the voices in my head and I can turn them off if I so desirer.

I have also learned, when I talk to myself, at least two intelligent people are in the conversation. This is much more than I can say about calling Disability.

Chapter 6: Comedy—How to Piss Off 4,338 people in 4,333 Words[1]

I started doing comedy over twenty years ago. My first

experience with seeing live comedy was a [redacted to save

a career] show in San Francisco. I enjoyed the first fifteen

minutes of her set. She opened with a scripted set, and then

---

[1] I know some of you BBs are going to count the words in this chapter. Go
ahead. I did.

asked the audience, "What do you all want to talk about?" I looked around and started counting the seats and doing the math. I thought, "Wow! I think you should have something to talk about. I paid $50 for my cheap seat, which by the way is located next to God." There was about 2,300 seats here going for $50 to $150, which works out to be approximately $23,000 (plus or minus a few dollars) a show. This was the second show that night. I believe that you will make around $30,000 for two sixty-minute routines; you should have something to talk about. Don't ask the audience. This is not *Who Wants to Be a Millionaire*. This was the first time I realized I could do what she did and make a good living. I tried not to leave bitter but I was deeply disappointed with the first comedy show I attended.

***

Comedy is not as easy as it appears. It takes hard work and practice; it is a job before it becomes a career. The best comedians have learned how to perfect their performances. They know how to work the audience and adjust their sets to fit any audience regardless of age, race, or other demographics.

Comedy has a big learning curve. So many of us see someone cracking jokes on stage and think, "Well, I could do that!" For people who have been told by friends and relatives "You are so funny! You should be a comic!" they really believe that professional stand-up is just getting up on stage and doing what you have been doing in the comfort of your own family reunion or office break room. Those people face a rude awakening if they try comedy.

Stand-up, good stand-up, involves a whole set of unique skills that are not employed when you chat with your friends at a bar. Just being funny isn't enough. You need to be funny on demand. For example you might need to be funny on Tuesday night at the comedy club for 45 minutes because that is your career. Even if you ate some nachos from the gas station across the street that has your stomach talking more than your mouth. You have no sick days. That is why some comics become BB'S and soon quit the world of comedy. I have seen my share.

Comedy is a job beyond being funny on stage. It involves understanding the business. Like your regular nine-to-five gigs, it requires understanding hierarchy, cliques, unwritten rules, and the business side of the job. The most successful comics are not always the funniest comics.

At the risk of forever being blacklisted, I am going to reveal some of the secrets of the stand-up world.

Unlike most jobs, stand-up doesn't require a formal interview to get up on stage. It doesn't have a set application or require a SOQ, statement of qualifications. This gives inexperienced folks the idea that just anyone can do stand-up. However, there is an actual set of required skills and knowledge involved in being a good stand-up comic.

A Statement of Qualifications (SOQ) is a statement representing the potential employee's experience that would qualify them for the job. And these questions do not necessarily get to the heart of why you are interested in this position. Can you be depended on to complete your job with a good attitude? Many applicants cannot answer basic questions honestly. Thinking and answering honestly would often result in answers like "The only reason I'm interested in this job is because I need the money and it pays more than the one I currently have" or "I can be reliable and have a good attitude as long as it is not a Monday or any day that requires me to talk to the people in the office."

Most of us lie on job applications and during the interview process because the reason we want the job is we need money.

If there was an interview to do comedy and comics had to answer the basic question of, "Why do you want this job?" You probably would get an answer like, "Because I think I am funny and expect to get a big break in the first eighteen months and then I tell everyone to suck it."

If they were asked "What inspired you to do stand-up comedy?" the reply might be "I was drunk with my friends, and we thought it was a good idea. So I made a bet and here I am, Mr. Funnyman at your service".

The hard skills that are necessary to become successful are ignored.

Successful comics can draw a lot of people out to a venue to see them. They can promote effectively. They can manage their money. They have acquired the soft skills to get along with other performers, bookers, and club owners - all of whom might be mean on stage, flake on payments, or screw you over and still expect you to come to the next show and bring a crowd.

In my experience, most people who try stand-up don't have the necessary skill set to be successful. They don't want to put in the work developing websites, Twitter followings, and YouTube channels; and they don't want to follow up with bookers and promoters about possible jobs.

They also are too sensitive to take criticism and instead of trying to improve, they choose to melt down on social media.

I learned early in the game that you have to be polite and professional if you want to succeed in this game. I worked for a prominent booker in my area (that has died. Not to speak ill of the dead, but…). When I did a show for this man, I caught the Bitter Bitch virus. The show itself was fine. I got bitter because the man booked me, made money off of my performance, and then would not pay me for weeks at a time.

He always had an excuse for nonpayment. "I have been sick *cough*." "Oh, I'm out of town." "I'll get it to you next week." While these may be legitimate excuses in some circumstances, when you work in comedy are on the road you need to be reimbursed in a timely manner.

 Sometimes you are paid in cash; mainly you are paid by check after you have finished your show. Yes by check after you have finished the show. This requires one to use their own money for traveling to and home from the show. Many times the club will feed you, or supply you with a card for food to be used in the club.

One the booker named in the above paragraph did not pay in a timely manner. This occurred around Christmas. He sent me one of his many excuses for not being able to pay and then posted a photo on Facebook posing with his Corvette with the caption "I need to put my baby away for the winter." It made me wonder if he could use his baby to drive to the post office and mail my check. I was becoming a bitter bitch fast.

He didn't owe me much for two shows. I was raising two kids and trying to make Christmas decent for them. While this was clearly no big deal to him, He could afford his Corvette, but he couldn't afford to pay me. I had traveled to Oregon and did the gig. I paid for the gas and rented the car. It took him more than a month to pay me. It's hard working for a Comedy pimp.

Cliques

I learned early that comedy is segregated. There are always haters in every game, and the haters are alive and well in the comedy. Some will show you their true colors up front, while others wait until you turn your back.

Comics are bad at keeping their mouths shut. Whether they do it to your face or just on their Facebook wall, all comics will show their true feelings sooner or later.

Comics are not united in one giant love-fest with each other. We organize by cliques:

- male versus female
- young versus old
- black versus white
- Hispanic versus white
- black female versus black male
- white female versus other females

Cliques tend to support their own, whoever that might be. Between cliques there is rivalry. Within cliques, there is jealousy. Comedy, I found, is a breeding ground for BB's and BBP's.

The Rules

Sometimes comedians think there are no rules, but there are rules in everything we do in life. Some rules are spoken and some unspoken. As soon as you break unspoken rules, you will know because everyone will start talking about the individual who broke the unspoken rules. Ask Ms. K&%$$ G@#&^%$. (too soon?) Nah! She broke the unspoken rules a she is paying dearly. She is somewhere being quite and hoping people forget about her. Don't call it freedom of speech because speech is not always free. We pay for things we say in some way or another. She lost and will lose many shows. But more importantly she lost the respect of comics and future up and coming comics.

Comedy is a selected job. No one is forced to do comedy on stage. Many of us do it because we love the art of comedy. I have found throughout my years—and I may say years—of doing comedy. There are a lot of haters among us, or BB's and BBP's. Yes, they may clap and say you had a good set. This might be totally true, but inside they are wishing you great failure because to see you go down is to see themselves come up.

I have made many mistakes when it comes to this side of the world of comedy. I have said things in a way I found helpful only to have a comedian twist it. For example, I told one person, maybe you should try to memorize your material. Writing notes on a glass or napkin is not fooling anybody. Plus, I went on; I think you have been doing the same material for about five years

You should know it, you have not changed it. So why can't you remember it? DUH?

Oh, can you say butt hurt? This comic cried foul and has talked so much trash behind my back that I know it to be backlash. But you see there is a difference between her behavior and mine, because at least I told this to her face. I posted on Facebook about a five-minute set she did, and there were several comments that went from left field to the football field. Why? Because they were trying to defend her. In the Sacramento comedy scene it might be okay to use notes, but just make sure you and your notes stay here in Sacramento, because you cannot do an open mic in LA with notes unless you are somebody famous and working on new material. Anyway, is that what we are in this for? To be famous? To make large amounts of money and quit our jobs, buy expensive cars and houses, eat at fancy restaurants, have little foo foo dogs and everything we desire? Is this it? Or are we doing comedy as a hobby?

I found out that I had trespassed on unspoken boundaries once this post went up on Facebook. All of a sudden, the black comedienne made the white comedienne cry. There was nothing motivated by race about this issue. There was nothing based in gender. Nevertheless, racial differences and both of us being women came into play. Apparently, as a female comic, I am supposed to refrain from criticizing other women. Additionally, I was black, she was white…and the comedy world is really racist. So, it became a race issue.

Why did she cry? I have no idea. I just said what I thought was true. The white female comics rallied around this woman to support her inability to remember five minutes of material. I was portrayed as the bad guy for criticizing her style on stage. Now I am isolated from the white comedienne click. I am not a BB because of this action. I knew they did not like me. To be labeled a BB I would have had to be disappointed by the white female comediennes click for ostracizing me from their group. I have always accepted that I am a lone ranger in this comedy world where I live.

Comics are not known for having backbones and thick skin. Instead of confronting someone, chatting about an issue, and resolving it in a professional manner, comics opt to ignore the individual who upset them. I soon became the Invisible Woman. This was amazing to me. It's not as if you can miss me standing with a bunch of white girls, but they can all somehow seem to look right through me as if I am a shadow.

There are plenty of times in my life when I wanted to be invisible. However, the power of invisibility occurs only when you don't need it. I did not make the comments out of anger or bitterness. To me, this was just an observation I found to be true. Apparently, the truth did not set this comic free. It just provided me with an inopportune cloak of invisibility.

If you want to grow as a comedian, you must be able to develop a thick skin and accept and incorporate critique and criticisms. This is why I don't understand people who go into comedy who were bullied in life. They are setting themselves up to be criticized again. Crying about the difficulties of being bullied and not fitting in is what group therapy is for, not comedy. Want to whine about your struggles in life? Become a poet. They love that stuff (cue sounds of fingers snapping in a coffee house).

Comedy Is a JOB

Some comedians are doing comedy as a hobby. Yet there are so comedians who desire to be a professional. Where do you draw line from open mic-er to feature, it is not at the point where you quit your day job. There is a business side of comedy. The business side is different today than twenty years ago. The successful comedians are not always the funniest ones. Just look around. They are the smartest ones. They did the most hustling. They did not take the state-worker approach.

Successful comics study the craft, write constantly, work their stuff out on stage, read about it, and live it. You do not do this job for the benefits or to be able to sit home and smoke weed all day. Honestly, if you are home enough to water your plants, you are not doing this comedy thing right.

There Are a Lot of Haters

Sometimes the haters are other comics who tend to bring down the other comedians or the entire mood. In many ways, the local comedy scene resembles high school, with alcohol involved.

There are Bitter Bitches in comedy. They arrive at shows and open mics with negative attitudes. They tell the stories of how great they were at the past mic, complaining that still the bookers don't like them for some reason. The BB comics always think their inability to book gigs has to do with personal beefs, not the fact that they can't fill seats or write decent material.

Male comics tend to have groupies, or "chuckle fuckers": audience members who want to have sex with them because women tend to think funny and sexy are related.

Male chuckle fuckers are less common. I believe it is because men are afraid that female comics will make fun of their penis, and that little dude is really the most sensitive little prick I have even met. This gender dynamic changes the rules for female comics. Male comics have much broader leeway in their appearance. They can be old and schlubby or young and hard bodied. Their looks don't impact their ability to book shows or draw an audience. Female comics have a much more narrow option for looks. If you are hot, it is a distraction and can actually hurt you in comedy. Comics are supposed to feel approachable. If you are the hot chick in the bar, guys get intimidated.

Women also have to be careful about sexuality on stage. Too little or too much can be a turnoff for an audience. Further, this is still a boy's-club profession. If you sleep with another comedian, a booker, an agent, or an audience member and you are found out (and you will be, because comics gossip like old yentas) you are seen as sleeping your way to the top.

It is not uncommon for female comics to be hit on by male comics. If there is one single rule to never break in comedy, it is this: never ever, ever have sex with another comedian. It only ends badly. You will become a part of his act on and off stage. It does not matter if the sex was good or bad. You will be a joke on stage—or worse, just a setup and not even the punch line.

Headliners

Comics who headline are a sensitive bunch. Many have strange personal rules for who they want to work with. My experience with female headliners is that they are the most two-faced comedians you will meet. They will say "We women need to stick together, because the men are not giving us our props!" They will go all "Gurl Power Unite!" when they are with a group of other comediennes, then tell the booker, "I do not want any females on the show with me."

This need to be the only female on the bill is driven by the desire to stand out and be the star of the show. A second woman on the bill distracts from the attention that might be lavished on them. This is the classic female-versus-female struggle. I try to understand this point of view, but I think if you do "you," and you are the star, why worry about the female opener? She is just trying to break into the big time, as you did. She can't steal your shine, so stop being a muff block, and encourage other women to be on your show.

It's Personal

I have shown up for shows and then read a list of rules that pertained only to me. For example, a booker will feel the need to inform me that, "This is a highly intelligent crowd. Do not do any sexual (i.e., pussy or dick) jokes. Many times this set of rules comes from bookers and comics who have not taken the time to Google me, YouTube my sets, or look at my website. I just agree with this. I try not to do blue (R-rated) comedy; that is not a part of who I am. Now, I am not saying I won't go into the land of Dick if a show necessitates it, but I choose not to make those types of jokes if at all possible. I have enough material that does not lead me down the stereotyped road of the Dirty Black Female comic. If you want to hire a raunchy black or white woman comedienne, I have a list of people who would be happy to do your show.

> *I have enough material that does not lead me down the stereotyped road of the Dirty Black Female comic.*

Many times I am stereotyped into that world just because of my skin color. I accept that being black will lead to this type of stereotyping. It is not that it is right or I think its okay, but it is so common, I expect it.

A white female comedienne will not be told to "avoid the dick jokes" as she is handed a microphone. Apparently, the idea that "white" and "clean" go together is so ingrained in us that white comediennes are assumed to have clean sets.

The degrading comments that males think they need to express before giving me a chance to perform on their show become tiresome and infuriating at times. It always amazes me, because anyone slightly familiar with my sets knows I can be the one with the cleanest material. However, I am the one who is approached with the "clean" rules—rules that no one thought about until the black female comic showed up. As much as people in a comedy industry try to say, "Oh we are all just comedians. There is no white or black, male or female, gay or straight, young or old," this has never been true. These divisions are real, and your reception as a comic is partially based on your ability to refute or fulfill a stereotype.

Getting Paid

Many comics have tried to make the transformation from open-mic comic to professional, paid comic. It's a difficult transformation to make. When do you call yourself a professional comedian?

People who get into open-mic comedy dream of being famous, having their own special, and headlining around the world. However, very few open-mic comics are willing to put in the time, the studying, and the work to make this happen.

Twenty years ago, comics dreamed of performing at a local open mic, having a famous booker or headliner come to the show, and getting their big break. Most people are not that naive about their big break now, but they are still looking for a shortcut. Now, instead of dreaming of a big break, beginning comics will try to ride the coattails of a successful local comic. This comic kissing up means that even a modestly successful local comic can always get on someone's show. The hope of the comic producing the show is always, "If so-and-so is on my show, she will feel the need to reciprocate for her next big gig!" Just putting the comic on a show you produce all the time does not guarantee you the same success.

I've learned that sucking up really doesn't pay, all the time. So don't be mad if I don't slow my roll because professional comics entered into the room. They are no different than me. Actually, strike that. Most of them are white.

Going Racial

Racial stereotype jokes are easy to write. They work well with a receptive audience, but try one with the wrong audience and you will be yelling "Start the car!" These jokes are not taken well if you insult the race you are trying to create a joke about. My thoughts about race jokes are to just make sure you are doing the jokes in front of the correct people. Otherwise leave it alone because you will offend somebody.

Final Thoughts

Comedy has bought a lot of people into my life. Some have changed my thinking about life, both for the good and bad. I've made a variety of friends: young, old, white, black, straight, and otherwise. I've met different people throughout the country ready to laugh and have fun. It is a great experience to share laughter with people of all races, because laughter is the one thing we can do together.

I learned the unspoken rules of comedy by breaking them. I am an individual who speaks my mind and will call out a comic (or really anyone) I think is being inappropriate or exhibiting bad behavior. Sometimes the Grey Goose encourages me to say it, and sometimes I just say it. If I did not mean what I said, I apologize, but drinking just makes me more honest. Even when I am a bit intoxicated, I probably meant it if I said it. Alcohol is just a good buddy encouraging me to say what is on my mind.

One of my biggest transgressions was commenting about a comic's apparent inability to work without notes. I was working with this female comic who cannot remember her set if her life depended on it. I have seen her set so many times I can recite it at four a.m. on my way to the bathroom. First I wrote a post on Facebook about remembering your material. I then wrote a drunken post on Facebook about memorizing your material, which turned into a long bitch fest. She thought I was being negative about her material. I did not comment on her material, I commented on her inability to remember her material. I don't know where it took a left turn, but now she sees me as her enemy.

What she fails to see is that the comics who tell her she has a great set and refuse to give constructive feedback are really hindering her. Why would you think its okay to carry notes on stage for a five-minute set that you've been doing for over five years? Her friends tell her that this is acceptable. However, in the larger and more professional comedy clubs, the stated rules are: no notes and no f-bombs. This is true at most clubs in Los Angeles, New York, Chicago, and other A-level venues a comic wants to break into. You are expected to do two or three minutes of "G"-rated material *and no notes*!

Whhaaat?! You can't bring notes on stage? She acted like this was a shocking fact. Hiding notes on a napkin wrapped around a glass and hoping no one notices is not a solution. If you want to get better, play bigger, and be respected, you need to be able to remember a five-minute set. And honestly, if you can sing along to your favorite song on the radio, you are three-fifths of the way to memorizing five minutes.

A sycophant will tell you this looks amazing. Only a real friend will tell you to let it go.

Chapter 7: Authentic Friends vs. Sycophants

*W*hen I play the game "What superpower would you want to have?" I never really have to think about it. I have been blessed and cursed with the power of invisibility. I would rather have the power of a white woman.

The power of a white woman, you ask? Yes, I want the power of a white woman. You see, a white woman is visible, she is desired, and she has the power to get the white man, who has money and power. She can worry about things like pumpkin-spice lattes not being in season and which yoga class to go to on her lunch hour. I want those types of worries.

Instead, I was given the power of invisibility. Over the years, I have found that only some people can see me. I divide these into two categories: authentic friends and sycophants.

Authentic friends are the friends who are there because they care about you, they like you, they don't need anything from you. These are the people who will have your back in a pinch. These are the folks you enjoy drinking with and who don't get offended at your "power of a white woman" joke.

Then there are sycophants. These are folks who see you only because they think you can facilitate them getting something they want. They make friends with you on the job because they think you will give them inside information about the boss or about a promotion opportunity. These are the comics who see you only until they realize you will not be booking them on all your future shows. When this reality sets in, you become so invisible they will accidently sit on you when searching for a place to land during an open mic.

Sometimes it can be hard to distinguish between an authentic person and a sycophant in the beginning. A sycophant will show up, ask how you are, and ask about you shows and work. I was always told you can't choose your family but you can choose your friends. So pick your friends wisely.

When you get to be over forty, true friends are hard to find. For some reason, by the time you reach forty you have either filled up all the "close friends" slots in your life or you just cannot seem to meet people you want to chill with. Bonding and trust are always hard, but by forty you have been burned enough to make trusting another adult a true challenge.

However, in this day and age when we move, change careers, have kids grow up and leave home, we have the need and opportunity to make new friends as adults. You know for sure when you have found a real friend. There is a gut feeling that you have met a person you connect with and can trust. True friends show up for your shows even though you didn't comp them the ten-dollar ticket. These are the people who will text you when they are not looking for a favor. These are the people who remember your birthday without a Facebook notice!

Invisibility

My power of invisibility is similar to the powers of a character just beginning to study magic in a Harry Potter novel. I don't have a lot of control over when it comes and goes.

I would love to be invisible when the bill collectors or Scientologists show up at my door. If I could wiggle my nose and become invisible and slip out during someone's bad set at a show or during a contentious family dinner, that would be amazing. But alas, I can't seem to control my invisibility. Other people have that power.

I seem to become very invisible at the local Bel Air deli. I don't know exactly why men who slice meat and cheese for a living don't see me, but they don't. I guess I don't look like a ham hock or a lump of roast beef.

I have gone into the Bel Air deli to grab lunch on several occasions. One afternoon I had been gardening and wanted to grab lunch. I washed my hands and such, but I was still wearing my gardening clothes when I ran over to the store. There was a line of four of us.

Now, my Bel Air does not have a regimented line or a "take a number" system. It is more of an honor system to get your American cheese slices. People notice who is there when they arrive and who comes after them. When the deli guys ask, "Who's next?" the right person steps forward.

So I am there. I am a bit grungy, but not like "house shoes outside the house" grungy. I am second in line. The deli guy calls for the next person, and I start to step up. He looks past me and helps another white woman in line. I speak up that I was next. He proceeds to help the other woman and then look confused as to who might possibly be next.

I understand the way light works. It was probably bouncing off her pale-ass arms, and he saw it first or something. But I also spoke up, and he fully ignored me. And I do resent being treated like I am a ringing phone and Apathetic Andrew is on staff.

This may seem petty or small, but when you are passed over again, and again, and again, the world becomes annoying and then hostile. Look, I am here. I have my money I was going to spend on your cold cuts. I clearly have the time to garden in the middle of the week when these other folks still have to bust their ass for a paycheck. It would be nice if you could see me.

Authentic Friends and Sycophants

Meeting true friends in comedy is complicated. We are performers. We make up stuff onstage for a living. We are developing a professional and public persona. We lie. So when you meet other comics, it can be quite unclear if they are asking about how you are doing because they care or because they are hoping you will reveal you are stressed because your feature for a show dropped out and they can wedge their open-mic level but into a feature gig.

I have come up with shorthand for the sycophants in the word: the "use-ee" and the "user." I once tried to explain this to a fellow comedian by saying, "People always want something from you. There are very few who will say 'no problem' and really mean no problem." More often, individuals will say the favor was no problem, but they will bring up the favor as soon as you say you can't book them in your next gig or give them the name of your agent.

Watch Me Lie

The biggest lie I have ever told another comic was "That was a great set." Comics are thin-skinned folks for the most part (refer to chapter five for a refresher on this). When they ask about their set, they really just want to hear that they were great. Attempts at actual feedback are seen as hostile and degrading. There is a reason so many who attempt stand-up never make it past the "bringer show" or "new faces showcase" stage. I'm just saying.

Another common lie is "No, I didn't think you were out of control at the bar last week. I am sure that the bartender/producer/other comics are just overreacting." People soon forget that they too were once a newbie in this industry. Now that they have made it (well, they've featured once or twice) they become divas. They get drunk because their bar tab is comped. They order sixty dollars' worth of chicken wings and assume the producer will cover it. They don't tip the wait staff.

Here is a big tip: just because it is free, you do not have to try to drink up an entire bottle of Johnnie Walker before your ten-minute set. Show a little decorum. Wait until you get into your private space to get drunk, smashed, and high or whatever you do to show your true self. Many of us are watching to see how professional you are.

Additionally, comics mistake sycophants for dating material. That cutie with the ten minutes and three laughs—well, she is not necessarily looking at you as a life partner. She might just be looking at you as the coattails she needs to ride to her next gig.

The rule of *don't sleep with a fellow comic* is broken regularly. It is an easy rule to break. You are in a bar or a club with these folks week in and week out. They make you laugh, and that is a turn-on for most of us. We won't have to go online to get a date! However, once the relationship breaks up, it's all bad. You become fodder for comedian gossip and new material in this person's act. And really, guys, you don't want her next dick joke to be about your smeckle.

When Sycophants Go Bad

Jail is a pretty big deterrent for me. If you have made it to adulthood and have not had to take a call from a friend who did something stupid and needs you to bail him or her out, well then, you aren't really living. I can honestly say I strive to always be the bail-or and not the bail-ee.

I took a road trip with a fellow comic whom I shall not name in this paragraph because I don't want to give her that much credit. My understanding of this trip was we would be going half on everything. Everything. This is normal. I rented the car, which we would split costs on, as well as gas and driving time. Well, before we left Sacramento, she asked me if I would mind if she smoked. I said, "No, as long as you don't smoke it in the car, because they will charge me for smoking in the car." She agreed, and we took off on a comedy road trip.

I took the first shift driving with the understanding we would change drivers when we made our first stop for gas. We stopped, and she went to smoke. When I said okay to smoking, I failed to realize that her choice of tobacco was the wacky kind.

She stepped aside and smoked her marijuana. I was not okay with this, because now I'm asking myself, "Does she expect to drive me in this fabulous Enterprise rental car high?" Look, I am old enough to die and not have people say, "But she was so young!" but I'll be damned if I'm going out because someone is too high to turn the wheel on a mountain road.

At this point I made an executive decision to continue to drive. We were four hours into the trip and still had a good five hours to go. I looked over at the passenger, and she was comfortable, looking out the widow stoned out of her mind. I soon noticed every time I stopped the car to stretch, she started smoking weed again, or "taking her medicine," as she described it to me. Look, as someone who manages chronic pain, I understand the need for medications that make it inadvisable to drive. But I choose to sober up if I have to be behind the wheel.

Nine hours later, we made it to the show. She was nice and relaxed, and I felt like a caged tiger. My nerves and my stress level were extremely high, and I was very tense. My back, neck, arms, legs, my whole body felt tight, and I could not stretch the muscles to relax. Sadly, since I don't partake of the green anymore, I could not dip into my rider's stash.

The show went well as far as I was concerned. I got paid. I met a few people. I sold a t-shirt, and an unnamed source (not riding with me) gave me some medical marijuana for my pain. Even though I do not smoke.

While I do not smoke, Wendy had no issue partaking on the ride home (look, I said I wouldn't name her in that one paragraph, not the whole book). I was the driver again, because Wendy woke up at three a.m. sick and then stayed in the bathroom until five o'clock throwing up and splashing around in the bathtub like Flipper, the stoned dolphin.

Because she booked the show, she gave away my room to another comic, and I had to share a room with her. ☹ I learned a lesson from all of this. I will never again agree to share a room. Pulling the diva card and saying you need privacy before a show both is necessary and can help save a friendship. When Wendy came out the bathroom at five a.m., I was awake, packed, and ready to leave. I couldn't sleep with all the splashing and retching taking place in the hotel bathroom. Look, I am a comic. I didn't sign up to tour with Keith Richards.

The drive was quiet until I made a bathroom stop at Target in Medford, Oregon. I went into Target to use the bathroom. I then started browsing through the store. I think I bought some chips and walked back outside.

It was probably eight in the morning. I came outside, and there she was, rolling a joint on the back of the rental car. I lost it. I asked her what she was doing; did she not see that Target had all type of cameras in this parking lot? As I was asking her this question, a young mother and her daughter looked at her and walked into the Target. She explained to me that weed is legal in Oregon and said I should not panic. Well, I was looking at her and said it was *not* okay; it was disrespectful to roll weed on the back of my rental car at eight in the morning in the Target parking lot. I didn't know what type of crazy she was. What I did know was that if the police were called, I would be the first one they would look at as a suspect for illegal activity. Going to jail in Medford, even for a few hours, was not on my bucket list.

The ride back from Medford, Oregon, was very quiet after I cussed her out. She had a few things to say, to which I told her she was totally stupid. She claimed I called her a bitch on the stage the previous night. In her defense, I probably did. I have called out more than one comic on stage. I have probably ruined a relationship or two with some offhand comments. However, I never say anything on stage I would not say to a person face to face (or now, in print form. Hello, fellow comics!).

Now, when I tell you that rolling weed on the back of a rental car in Oregon is a bad idea, what I really mean is, "Stupid bitch, don't roll weed on the back of the car. It's eight in the morning. These soccer moms aren't so down with you hitting a joint in front of the five-year-old."

The big conclusion from all of this is that in comedy, as in any workplace, you need to set boundaries. You also need to respect the boundaries of others. Yes, I appreciate being added to shows and getting paid for doing what I like doing. But I do expect others to be professional about the whole enterprise. If you are bringing me along to drive you for twenty hours, to risk entanglement with the police, it's going to cost a lot more than a shared hotel room in a two-star hotel and a couple hundred bucks. My time, my ass, and my car are worth more than that.

Authentic Friends

There are actual good people out there who are your real friends. These folks will like you for you. They are not looking to get a handout or to get on your gig or to be with you because they think you are popular and cool. They just like you. These people are special, and you should keep them close.

People have heard of love at first sight. I haven't experienced that, but I have known true friends at first sight. As happens with love at first sight, people you are destined to have a deep friendship with appear at odd and unexpected times. They are then in your life forever. Sycophants and Bitter Bitches are like this too, but they are more like a "burning bag of poo" surprise, and friends are more like a "fresh cookies in the break room" type of surprise.

I met a friend when I was interviewing for a job at the DMV. That right there made this weird. The DMV is not a place where anyone—customers, employees, homeless using the bathroom, anyone, really—is happy to be there. She worked with Biggie and Tupac (bossholes I have known). On my first day at the DMV, I stepped off the elevator and Karen was there and gave me a hug. (I told you this was a weird way to make a friend.) Once I figured out she had not tagged me with a tracking device or placed a "Kick Me" sign on my back, we became friends. We have been friends ever since.

That was over ten years ago, and the experience was great. The DMV was full of people, and before I left I developed a few friendships that I cherish to this day. Thanks, Karen, for not putting a "Kick me" sign on my back that first day! You are one of the friends I cherish.

I never expected to make good friends, let alone female friends, in comedy. The cliqueiness and competitive nature of the business tends to pit us against one another. But similarly to my friendship with Nina at the DMV, I made a friend in comedy in an unexpected way.

I got a chance to compete in a comedy completion called The She-Devil Competition, held in New York. It was a great opportunity, and I was thrilled to qualify as a top female comic.

As with many things in life—living on a beach, having a set of minions to do my bidding, enjoying tropical drinks served to me by a beautiful and shirtless man—the thing that stood in the way of my fantasy was money.

I was unsure how I was going to pay for the trip to NYC and afford things like a place to stay. You see, even when you qualify for a competition, the producers expect you to pay for the privilege of them making money on your performance.

A female comic, Daphnique, came to me and said, "Hey, you can stay with me. I already have a room." I was touched by her generosity but could not afford to pay half of the room. (See, I understand this isn't a free ride.) She was okay with it and let me stay with her for free. We had a great week in New York. The whole experience with Daphnique was special, and since we had met only a few days before this, I was floored by her generosity and kindness.

When we met, we had a vibe that I felt and she felt, and we knew we were going to be friends. She is also unique in that I don't need to pull the diva card and demand my own room for a show. I can't say that about just any comic.

As cynical as I can be, as many Bitter Bitches as I've encountered in my life, I can still be deeply touched when someone has my back without expectation of a returned favor.

Chapter 8: Don't Poison the Coffee

I have spent my life working in private industry and civil

service, and the one feature I find consistent in every job is

the bitter, passive-aggressive coworker. Bitter coworkers

find many ways to not do their job without getting fired. They bring their bad attitude into the office and spread it faster than the common cold. They make your job more difficult and attempt to infect you with their negativity.

I see examples of people dealing with bitter coworkers everywhere I go. While the syndrome is prevalent in civil service, it also manifests in private industry. I was in a large craft store recently. The phone began to ring. There were three cashiers up front, and only one had a customer. The phone rang and continued to ring. It looked as if the three cashiers were playing the age-old game of chicken with who would finally answer. When one did, the second one shook her head and muttered that the third never answered the phone. Clearly, this workspace had been infected with the BB virus.

Surviving and thriving in a work environment means learning to deal with these bitter colleagues. As black women, we face an extra challenge. Anytime we show annoyance at the bitter coworker, anytime we bring up the slacker to our manager, and anytime we ask the bitter colleague to adjust a behavior, we risk being seen as the Angry Black Woman. It's not fair. It's not true. But unfortunately, in most work environments, it is the reality of our world.

Race and gender will play into any situation at work, even when the issue at hand has nothing to do with race and gender. We are seen first as Black, second as a women, and third as anything else. Complaining about Michael not completing his assignment on time and delaying your work can be seen as being "uppity" and "aggressively" breaking the stereotype of operating on "Black-People Time." Talking to your supervisor about Susan's relentlessly negative attitude and its impact on your team can be seen as "infighting" amongst females.

Sometimes you need to speak up to address particularly bad situations. However, that is not always an option. Here are some tools I have learned over the years for dealing with bitter coworkers without being cast as the Aggressive Black Woman.

Self-Care

Taking care of yourself first is the most important thing. As women, we naturally tend to take care of everyone around us before addressing our own needs. Self-sacrifice can be deeply embedded in our behavior. This can also be very detrimental when you are dealing with a bitter coworker.

Self-care includes knowing when to walk away from a situation. It is often appropriate to excuse yourself and step into the ladies' room or go for a walk to discharge the negative energy that builds up from dealing with bad colleagues. Many times, it is not that staying would lead to confrontation. Rather, the negativity seeps into the space you are in, and you find yourself ruminating on angry thoughts or rehearsing what you fantasize about saying to the bad colleague. This is a great time to take a walk.

Self-care also means knowing when it is appropriate to speak the coworker or a supervisor. This is your job and your career. You need to protect your job. If a coworker's bad behavior is bleeding over and affecting your performance, it needs to be addressed.

While bitter employees tend to bank all their time off and see it as a badge of honor to never take a day off, there is no glory in bringing your sick or negative self into the office. Self-care can also include a day off. If you have vacation or sick days, sometimes you need to take one for mental-health reasons. Give yourself permission to take a day off, and do something to inoculate yourself against the BB virus.

Set Boundaries

There are things that are okay to do at work and things that are not okay to do in an employment setting. Bitter coworkers often cross these boundaries. The bad coworker will do stuff like fail to complete a task, then run to you for help and ask you not to mention it to anyone. Or this person will take great leeway with coming back from lunch, delaying your break on a regular basis. Or he or she simply will never pitch in for a task that multiple people are supposed to do.

These behaviors are not okay in a professional setting. You may feel the need to help the person out or not say anything to keep the peace in the office. However, you were not hired to be a doormat. When a coworker repeatedly crosses a basic work boundary, speak up.

Soften the Blow

In reality, you probably are not aggressive or angry on the job. However, non-Black supervisors and other employees tend to interpret what Black women do through a cultural lens that programs them to see us all as off-the-handle reality-television stars. Speaking softly and offering a critique that, in most cases, seems way too soft on the actual offender are often necessary so you don't scare the white people. You have to ease someone into hearing you.

Preemptively Protect Yourself

Always keep the idea that things will get racial fast in an employment situation. If the bad employee is not Black, there is a pretty good chance that your complaints or issues with this employee will be framed as a "cultural misunderstanding" or an attack on a person of another race. When you send e-mails about the employee to your supervisor or HR, keep records of these e-mails outside of the company e-mail server. When you talk to your supervisor or the employee, at the first mention of "culture" or "class" or "privilege" or you being "urban" (and the whole list of code words people use instead of saying "you're Black"), gently point out that your complaint has nothing to do with race or cultural understanding. Reiterate the actual issue. For example: "Simon is supposed to be back from lunch at one so I can take my lunch. He is rarely back before one fifteen, cutting into my lunch hour." Or "Susan hasn't sent me the weekly report due on Friday for the last six weeks, and I can't complete the next step." You have to continually remind people that people displaying bad work habits and being bitter have nothing to do with your skin color.

Check Your Head

You are your best defense against the BB virus. Just as you keep track of your physical health, you need to inoculate yourself against the bitter virus and regularly assess whether you are getting ill.

This is as simple as being conscious about how you feel in the morning on the way to work. Do you resent having to go into the office? Are you tired and forcing yourself to go in? Do you begin fighting with your coworkers in your head before you get through the front security doors? Do you want to cry?

These are signs you need a break or a new job. You have to be your first defense against bitterness and a bad attitude. Committing to a good attitude and a good day can help defend you against a bad job.

This is not saying all jobs are salvageable. Some jobs you will want to quit before the first smoke break. Some jobs are horrid. Some bosses are horrible. Some jobs can kill you. You may want to kill someone on those jobs. Those jobs need to go away, and you need something else.

Most jobs are tolerable. Reminding yourself that you will be nice to people, that you will work and be pleasant, can go a long way toward making your job and you more tolerable (e.g., ☺ I will remain happy for the next eight hours and twenty-seven minutes.).

Use Your Vacation and Sick Days

Don't be a hero. Spend your vacation and sick days. You have earned these days, and you need to use them. One of the most effective ways to make yourself more productive at work and enjoy it more (or at least hate it less) is to get out of the office once in a while.

Everyone hates the colleague who comes in with a head cold, then so generously shares it with the rest of the office. You do not want to be *that* employee. Everyone believes they will be punished if they take time off when ill. The reality is if you keep the office healthy by taking a day or two when you are on death's door with the flu, you will be more respected.

Vacations are also important. Everyone needs a break from the grind. Even when you do something you love for a living, you need to refresh yourself. Get out of the office. Turn off your office phone. Don't check your e-mail. Forget about the drama. You and your office will be better for your break.

Your Job Is Not Who You Are

Americans are obsessed with their jobs. We make our employer part of our identity. One of the most common questions asked of any new acquaintance is, "So, what do you do?"

This question never refers to what you do for fun, what your creative life goals are, or what you do to feed your soul. It is asked in reference to who employs you. And who employs you is part of who you are in this country.

This can be devastating for people. People who have not achieved a position they desire or who perceive they are in a low-status job often feel bad about themselves and what they do. Plenty of people who are trying to support their family by working at a large big-box store or working two part-time jobs in the fast-food industry are made to feel like failures because they are not one of the admired professionals: doctors, lawyers, or celebrities.

We tend to equate people's jobs with their personal qualities: doctors and professors are smart; lawyers are cunning; nurses and teachers are caring; comedians have mental illnesses. As with any stereotype, these things are not universally true. There are plenty of doctors who have average intelligence and plenty of teachers who are horrible people. But we categorize personalities based on profession.

The thing is we are no longer in a world where you work in one industry or with one employer for a lifetime. Most people have at least four career changes and multiple employers. In some industries today, if you are on staff for more than four years, people assume you are stagnating and have nothing left to offer.

You are also replaceable; DO NOT FORGET THIS. Most employers will fire you and only consider their bottom line and legal requirements for notifications and severance. Making your profession or your employer part of your relationship is like being in a one-sided relationship. If you say "I love you" and get "Cool" in response, you know it is not going to last. Accept your employment for what it is: a place to contribute for the time being, a building block in your career, and a way to make a little money.

Engage Outside of Work

Humans are creatures of habit and creatures of comfort. However, we are also social beings. We actually need interaction and stimulation from other people to keep our brains happy and healthy.

The need to be social and the need to do something routine and comfortable leads people to engage socially with people in the workplace. Don't get me wrong; having a drink with coworkers every now and then can help lubricate the office functioning. You do need to eventually develop a life outside the office.

I know that saying "Pick a night to go out and do something with people you *don't* work with" can feel like adding a chore to your already overburdened life. This chore, however, is actually more necessary than your run to Costco or yet another night staying in and binging on Netflix.

Engaging with people outside the office opens up your world. You are in the office with people in your same industry. You have similar social norms and similar time demands. You probably have similar outlooks on the world.

When you start to have friends outside the office, you can discover entirely new ways of looking at the world. For example, if I had stayed at the DMV and socialized only with people who also worked at the DMV, I might have developed a belief that everyone else in the world was a belligerent idiot who demanded that we poor, put-upon government workers do outrageous things like enter data correctly, move at a pace closer to human speed instead of sloth speed, and smile once in a while. Socializing with just work people eventually leads to an "us" against "everyone else" view of the world. You need to break that mold.

Additionally, people are attracted to an industry for a variety of reasons. There are personality types that fit better with some jobs and in some industries. If you enjoy being creative and finding solutions, you might fit well in a nonprofit but be a poor fit for government work. If you enjoy bossing people around, believe you are smarter than God, and don't think anyone else in the world but you has anything important to offer, well, a career as a surgeon or judge might be a good fit. You might also want to consider taking a job at the disabilities-service office in claims processing.

Socializing outside a group that is like you forces you to learn new ways of communicating, sheds light on how other people think about things, and opens doors. It is unlikely you will find your dream spouse or BFF in the office. Improve your world, and get out of your cube.

Learn to Fight Fair, Office Style

Reality television has glorified nasty, bitter fighting. You will never see a promo for a reality-television show that says, "Tonight, on *Real Dance-Mom Cat Hoarders*, Tammy discovers she made a mistake and apologizes from the heart, then seeks to make things better. Christian talks about how great his monogamous, loving marriage has been. And the kids clean their rooms without too much whining."

We have turned brutal, hurtful fighting into our nightly entertainment. Growing up, most of us did not actually see how our parents managed strife at work. Instead, we grew up thinking that S.O.B. was the correct spelling of "boss" and that Sheila in accounting was really a two-faced slut who couldn't process a paycheck to save her life. We enter the work world not knowing how to fight in an office.

There are things to fight for at work. You need to learn to stand up for yourself, to confront coworkers, and to protect yourself in a mature, adult, professional way. You also need to let some issues go. You don't figure out how to do this until you are actually in the work world.

Fighting unfairly in the workplace leads to acrimony, animosity, and sometimes being fired. It makes us dread going into work and has negative physical impacts like high blood pressure, weight gain, and anxiety. Learning to fight fair helps prevent these negative impacts.

Fighting fair has several key parts:

- Know what hills to die on.
- Know how to assert yourself kindly.
- Know the rules for your job.
- Never use personal attacks.
- Ultimately, know that it is about the work, not you.

Not every office battle is worth fighting. A mature, stable employee is one who knows which battles to take on and which ones to simply let lie. You learn that it actually isn't important that Jody never takes a turn changing the water bottle on the cooler. It *is* important that you figure out how to help Dave get his copyediting done so you can move your report forward. Every job will have different things to fight about. Your goal needs to be figuring out if something is really important or not.

Knowing how to assert yourself is important. Bursting into your boss's office and demanding a raise with no justifications three months after you just got a raise is not useful. Figuring out how to present your boss with information that you are underpaid and should reasonably be given more money is critical for successful employment.

You also need to set boundaries in the office. It might be okay for John to ask you to look over a one-page document for grammar and spelling errors. It is another thing for Jillian to ask you to edit the sci-fi novel she wants to self-publish. Letting your boss and coworkers know what is okay to ask you to do and what is not will go a long way toward making the office tolerable.

You have to assert yourself in the right way. Often, saying "no" or "I can't" isn't an acceptable option. Asserting boundaries in the office often involves short explanations of why you will or will not do something. Saying "I will edit your novel for $500. I am a professional writer, and this is my job. I am happy to do it, but I won't do it for free" is very different than "Bitch, please! I am not going to read your shitty *Doctor Who* fan fiction!"

You need to understand the rules of your workplace. Fighting fair means playing by the rules. If it is standard to involve a manager with small disagreements between coworkers, then notify her. If people settle small issues themselves, then do it that way.

This bleeds into the next rule: do not attack someone on personal issues. If your beef with a coworker is based on who she is as a person, this is not a workplace fight. Hate her perfume? That is your issue. Worried that he might be smoking marijuana on the weekends because you think you smell it on him, but his performance isn't impacted? That is a personal issue, not a work issue. None of these are worth elevating to a work fight.

The bottom line is that problems at work have to be about work. You can hate someone's politics, the way he talks about his kids, the way she dresses or styles her hair. This is your issue, not a work issue.

If he is doing something that makes the work suffer, then it is time to address it. If her frequent tardiness impacts your ability to do your job, it is time to assert yourself and deal with the issue. If his attitude is toxic to the environment, you need to address it. You need to begin to draw barriers between work and life and keep work at work.

Laugh at It

Some things at work are so ridiculous you just have to laugh. You could yell and cry and get frustrated, but it will never help.

A friend of mine works in the creative industries. The company does not drug test and does not have a "drug-free" policy. She had to talk to her assistant about the need to clean off her coke ring after she snorted blow in the bathroom before coming back to her desk.

Yes, she had to tell her employee to be discrete about using cocaine in the office. This is not something most jobs in management prepare you for. However, the assistant was more productive after a bump of coke, and her work improved for a short period of time, so my friend couldn't make the drug use a performance issue.

Sometimes you just have to laugh at the absurdity of your life. That is what I did with all the Bitter Bitches who crossed my path. They were horrible to work with. They caused me a bit of strife. Ultimately, however, I survived and then thrived. And without all the outrageous, crazy crackheads, drama queens, and apathetic IT folks who crossed my path, I wouldn't have a solid hour of comedy I could do on stage.

Don't let the Bitter Bitches get you down. Instead, reframe and accept that your job is just a job. Your job is not your life. You are bigger than your job. Life is so much greater than what you do from nine to five. If you are lucky, you can turn that BB into a great story!

Dealing with the Bitter Bitches, email me your story:

http://www.Workingwiththebbs.com

Thank you

I would like to say thank you to God and my parents for making this all possible, and for blessing me with my two wonderful children Andrea and Alex. You two mean the world to me. A special thank you to my wonderful grandsons Peter and Preston Best you two are great. Remember you will get a job interview with those names. It's on you to get the job.

I would like to extend a special thank you to my fans and to all the folks that help me make this book imaginable. Many of you have helped me in a way that only you and I can understand. Thank you Kul for talking on the phone with me as I drove to work knowing that I hated every minute of the travel and my final destination. Thank you Rebecca, Cousin Dina, Tanya, Luenell, Kat, Shelby, Shea, Nina, Denise, Greg and Yolanda, for you all contributed in ways that I might only understand but "Thank you".

And most of all "Thank you" to my pastor and my church family. I love you all. If I forgot you please except my apology this book has been a long road traveled.

About the Author

Sinn D. Rella is a working comic based in Sacramento, California. She graduated from the Oregon State University, the home of the Beavers. She has a degree in sociology, which has proven to be immensely useful in both the work world and comedy. She has two grown children and finally a washer and dryer that match! Her comedy largely involves pointing out the absurdities in life and naming those things we all experience but don't have the words to talk about (e.g., the Bitter Bitch). You can find out more about Sinn at www.workingwiththebbs.com.